LAFAYETTE

Famous Crimes of
the 20th Century

CRIME, JUSTICE, AND PUNISHMENT

Famous Crimes of the 20th Century

WITHDRAWN

Alan Marzilli

Austin Sarat, GENERAL EDITOR

CHELSEA HOUSE
PUBLISHERS

A Haights Cross Communications ✚ Company

Philadelphia

Frontis: *Clyde Barrow in front of car with a gun collection.*

Chelsea House Publishers
Editor in Chief Sally Cheney
Director of Production Kim Shinners
Creative Manager Takeshi Takahashi
Manufacturing Manager Diann Grasse

Staff for FAMOUS CRIMES OF THE 20TH CENTURY
Editor Lee Marcott
Production Assistant Jaimie Winkler
Picture Researcher Sandy Jones
Series and Cover Designer Takeshi Takahashi
Layout 21st Century Publishing and Communications, Inc.

A Haights Cross Communications Company

First Printing

1 3 5 7 9 8 6 4 2

The Chelsea House World Wide Web address is
http://www.chelseahouse.com

Library of Congress Cataloging-in-Publication Data

Marzilli, Alan.
    Famous crimes of the 20th century / By Alan Marzilli.
        p. cm.
Includes index.
Summary: Describes some of the major crimes committed in the United
States during the twentieth century and discusses the social impact of
these criminal acts and the trial and punishment of the perpetrators.
    ISBN 0-7910-6788-2
    1. Crime—United States—History—20th century—Juvenile literature.
[1. Crime—History—20th century.] I. Title.
HV6783 .M35 2002
364.973'09'04—dc21

                                                            2002007533

Contents

CRIME, JUSTICE, AND PUNISHMENT

Fears and Fascinations:

An Introduction to
Crime, Justice, and Punishment

By Austin Sarat

We live with crime and images of crime all around us. Crime evokes in most of us a deep aversion, a feeling of profound vulnerability, but it also evokes an equally deep fascination. Today, in major American cities the fear of crime is a major fact of life, some would say a disproportionate response to the realities of crime. Yet the fear of crime is real, palpable in the quickened steps and furtive glances of people walking down darkened streets. At the same time, we eagerly follow crime stories on television and in movies. We watch with a "who done it" curiosity, eager to see the illicit deed done, the investigation undertaken, the miscreant brought to justice and given his just deserts. On the streets the presence of crime is a reminder of our own vulnerability and the precariousness of our taken-for-granted rights and freedoms. On television and in the movies the crime story gives us a chance to probe our own darker motives, to ask "Is there a criminal within?"

as well as to feel the collective satisfaction of seeing justice done.

Fear and fascination, these two poles of our engagement with crime, are, of course, only part of the story. Crime is, after all, a major social and legal problem, not just an issue of our individual psychology. Politicians today use our fear of, and fascination with, crime for political advantage. How we respond to crime, as well as to the political uses of the crime issue, tells us a lot about who we are as a people as well as what we value and what we tolerate. Is our response compassionate or severe? Do we seek to understand or to punish, to enact an angry vengeance or to rehabilitate and welcome the criminal back into our midst? The CRIME, JUSTICE, AND PUNISHMENT series is designed to explore these themes, to ask why we are fearful and fascinated, to probe the meanings and motivations of crimes and criminals and of our responses to them, and, finally, to ask what we can learn about ourselves and the society in which we live by examining our responses to crime.

Crime is always a challenge to the prevailing normative order and a test of the values and commitments of law-abiding people. It is sometimes a Raskolnikov-like act of defiance, an assertion of the unwillingness of some to live according to the rules of conduct laid out by organized society. In this sense, crime marks the limits of the law and reminds us of law's all-too-regular failures. Yet sometimes there is more desperation than defiance in criminal acts; sometimes they signal a deep pathology or need in the criminal. To confront crime is thus also to come face-to-face with the reality of social difference, of class privilege and extreme deprivation, of race and racism, of children neglected, abandoned, or abused whose response is to enact on others what they have experienced themselves. And occasionally crime, or what is labeled a criminal act, represents a call for justice, an appeal to a higher moral order against the inadequacies of existing law.

Figuring out the meaning of crime and the motivations of criminals and whether crime arises from defiance, desperation, or the appeal for justice is never an easy task. The motivations and meanings of crime are as varied as are the persons who engage in criminal conduct. They are as mysterious as any of the mysteries of the human soul. Yet the desire to know the secrets of crime and the criminal is a strong one, for in that knowledge may lie one step on the road to protection, if not an assurance of one's own personal safety. Nonetheless, as strong as that desire may be, there is no available technology that can allow us to know the whys of crime with much confidence, let alone a scientific certainty. We can, however, capture something about crime by studying the defiance, desperation, and quest for justice that may be associated with it. Books in the CRIME, JUSTICE, AND PUNISHMENT series will take up that challenge. They tell stories of crime and criminals, some famous, most not, some glamorous and exciting, most mundane and commonplace.

This series will, in addition, take a sober look at American criminal justice, at the procedures through which we investigate crimes and identify criminals, at the institutions in which innocence or guilt is determined. In these procedures and institutions we confront the thrill of the chase as well as the challenge of protecting the rights of those who defy our laws. It is through the efficiency and dedication of law enforcement that we might capture the criminal; it is in the rare instances of their corruption or brutality that we feel perhaps our deepest betrayal. Police, prosecutors, defense lawyers, judges, and jurors administer criminal justice and in their daily actions give substance to the guarantees of the Bill of Rights. What is an adversarial system of justice? How does it work? Why do we have it? Books in the CRIME, JUSTICE, AND PUNISHMENT series will examine the thrill of the chase as we seek to capture the criminal. They will also reveal the drama and majesty of the criminal trial as well as the day-to-day reality of a criminal justice system in which trials are the exception and negotiated pleas of guilty are the rule.

When the trial is over or the plea has been entered, when we have separated the innocent from the guilty, the moment of punishment has arrived. The injunction to punish the guilty, to respond to pain inflicted by inflicting pain, is as old as civilization itself. "An eye for an eye and a tooth for a tooth" is a biblical reminder that punishment must measure pain for pain. But our response to the criminal must be better than and different from the crime itself. The biblical admonition, along with the constitutional prohibition of "cruel and unusual punishment," signals that we seek to punish justly and to be just not only in the determination of who can and should be punished, but in how we punish as well. But neither reminder tells us what to do with the wrongdoer. Do we rape the rapist, or burn the home of the arsonist? Surely justice and decency say no. But, if not, then how can and should we punish? In a world in which punishment is neither identical to the crime nor an automatic response to it, choices must be made and we must make them. Books in the CRIME, JUSTICE, AND PUNISHMENT series will examine those choices and the practices, and politics, of punishment. How do we punish and why do we punish as we do? What can we learn about the rationality and appropriateness of today's responses to crime by examining our past and its responses? What works? Is there, and can there be, a just measure of pain?

CRIME, JUSTICE, AND PUNISHMENT brings together books on some of the great themes of human social life. The books in this series capture our fear and fascination with crime and examine our responses to it. They remind us of the deadly seriousness of these subjects. They bring together themes in law, literature, and popular culture to challenge us to think again, to think anew, about subjects that go to the heart of who we are and how we can and will live together.

Introduction: The Trial That America Watched on TV

Football Star O.J. Simpson Found Not Guilty of Two Murders

On June 12, 1994, Los Angeles Police Department detectives were called to investigate what appeared to be a double homicide. Sadly, the LAPD investigated a lot of homicides—the city's violent gangs battled over territory and control of drug sales, and shootings were common. But these homicides were different: they happened in the city's wealthy Brentwood section, and the killings were particularly gruesome. An attractive woman, probably in her thirties, lay in a pool of blood, her head practically severed from her body. Nearby, an attractive man, probably younger than the other victim, also had his throat slashed. Both had multiple stab wounds, including cuts on their hands—probably from defending themselves from the attacker or attackers.

The bodies were found when a white dog, anxiously barking and with bloody paws, led startled neighbors to the scene. A horrible crime like this in such an upscale neighborhood was sure to attract attention, but police detectives knew that they had a major case on their hands when they identified the woman who had been killed. She was Nicole Brown, the ex-wife of O.J. Simpson.

Orenthal James Simpson, known to the world as "O.J.," or the "Juice" had first found fame in Los Angeles many years earlier when playing running back for the University of Southern California football team; he won the Heisman Trophy as the nation's top college football player in 1968. He then played professional football, at one time holding records for most rushing yards in a game and in a season. His celebrity status and good looks helped him launch a career in front of the camera, as a sportscaster, movie actor, and spokesman for Hertz rental cars.

The detectives on the scene would have the duty of notifying Simpson of the tragedy. But they had many other duties. They entered the house through a wide-open door; thankfully, Nicole's two children were safely asleep. Police officers took the children to the police station, making sure that they did not see the gruesome scene outside. They also began to collect evidence at the crime scene—clues that would help them find out who was responsible for these killings.

Soon, the crime scene was filled with detectives. Among the evidence they discovered were a bloody leather left-hand glove, a blue knit cap, bloody footprints, and a trail of blood droplets leading to the rear of the house. Nothing appeared to be stolen from the house; also, the victims' wallets were found, and Brown's Jeep and Ferrari were both parked at the house. The viciousness of the wounds confirmed that robbery was not the motive: whoever had killed the two was very angry.

A group of four officers left the crime scene to tell Simpson the horrible news. When they arrived at Simpson's walled mansion at around 5:00 A.M., a light was on, but nobody answered the buzzer at the gate. As

Evidence found at the bloody scene of the Brentwood murders began to lead investigators to suspect O.J. Simpson as the murderer. DNA testing further confirmed the detectives' suspicions.

the officers waited outside, one of them noticed what appeared to be blood on a white Ford Bronco truck parked outside the gate. Was it possible that the killers had gone after Simpson too? One of the detectives, Mark Fuhrman, scaled the five-foot wall and let the other officers pass through.

There was no answer at the front door of the house, and when the policemen went around to the back, they noticed three smaller houses on Simpson's property. In one of them was Arnelle Simpson, a daughter from O.J.'s first marriage, and in another was Kato Kaelin, an aspiring actor who was living there. Worried when neither of the two knew Simpson's whereabouts, the policemen asked Arnelle to let them into the house. They found no signs of a struggle, and for the moment thought that Simpson must be safe.

Arnelle then called her father's personal assistant, who told her that Simpson had flown to Chicago that night on an overnight flight and gave her the name of the hotel where he was staying. One of the detectives, Tom Lange, then pulled Arnelle aside and told her of the tragedy. A second detective, Ronald Phillips, called Simpson in Chicago as Kaelin was recounting his actions that night to Detective Philip Vannatter. Earlier, Kaelin had gone to McDonald's with Simpson, and brought food home with him. Later, at about 10:45 P.M., he heard a thud against his back wall. He went outside and saw a limousine driver waiting outside the gate. As the driver was telling Kaelin that he had been waiting for some time to take Simpson to the airport, Simpson came out of the house.

Meanwhile, Fuhrman had been outside ten to fifteen minutes looking for anything unusual behind Kaelin's back wall. What exactly happened outside would later become a matter of controversy, but when he returned, he led another detective to a bloody leather right-hand glove, much like the one found at the murder scene. As the sun rose, one of the detectives discovered what appeared to be a trail of blood leading from the white Bronco to the front door of the house. With this new evidence, the detectives decided to get a search warrant—a document approved by a judge that allows police to conduct a thorough search of private property.

When Simpson arrived home, television cameras were rolling. The story was already the top news item in the nation. During the entire investigation, members of the media were eager to film anything having to do with the case and to interview anyone who knew—or claimed to know—anything about the case. Because Simpson was involved both in entertainment and sports, the story was all over the newspapers, magazines, radio, and television.

Detectives Lange and Vannatter asked Simpson if he would come to the police station with them. He agreed. During their conversation, Simpson told a number of slightly different versions of what he had done the previous evening. He told them that he and Kaelin "went and got a burger, and I'd come home and kind of leisurely got ready to go," but then later said: "I was throwing hangers and stuff in my suitcase . . . Anybody who has ever picked me up says that O.J.'s a whirlwind at the end. He's running, he's grabbing things, and that's what I was doing." Simpson was also vague about how he had gotten a significant cut on his left hand. He first suggested that it might have happened in Chicago, when he broke a glass in his hotel room. However, after the detectives told him that they had found blood in the Bronco and on his driveway, he said that he must have cut his finger, "when I was rushing to get out of my house."

The detectives did not push Simpson too far because they wanted him to be cooperative in providing a sample of his blood—they hoped to test the blood to compare it to the blood found at Simpson's house and the crime scene. Simpson agreed, and a nurse filled a vial with Simpson's blood and also treated the cut on Simpson's finger. Vannatter took the vial of blood with him to Simpson's house so that he could give it to Dennis Fung, the expert who was collecting blood there. When Vannatter arrived, the cameras were still rolling, and they filmed him turning over the blood to Fung.

When the blood tests came back, the LAPD detectives thought that they had an open-and-shut case. Blood tests examine DNA (deoxyribonucleic acid), which is an extremely complicated chemical found in every living particle of the human body—including the blood. Like fingerprints, DNA differs from person to person. Blood tests use chemical "markers" that allow experts to compare one piece of DNA to another to see if they match. A test performed on one of the drops of blood found at the crime scene "showed that only one out of 57 *billion* people had those markers. Simpson was one of them. In other words, just on the blood evidence alone, there's only a one out of 57 billion chance that Simpson is innocent. Fifty-seven billion is approximately ten times the current population of the entire world." Additional tests indicated an extremely high probability that Brown and Goldman's blood was present on the glove collected outside Simpson's house, on socks found in his bedroom, and in his Bronco.

However, as the detectives and the rest of the world would soon learn, the American justice system does not determine guilt on blood evidence alone. It must be determined how the blood got to the crime scene through a trial, at which witnesses present evidence, a judge rules which evidence can be presented, prosecuting attorneys try to prove that the evidence proves guilt, defense attorneys try to prove that the evidence does *not* prove guilt, and a jury of twelve ordinary citizens decides whether the accused person is guilty or innocent.

With results of the blood tests in hand, the police were ready to arrest O.J. Simpson, and the prosecutors were

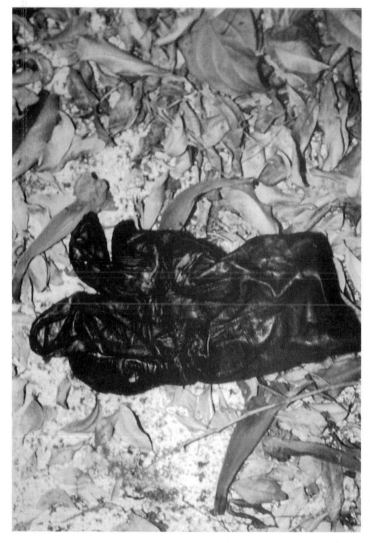

An important piece of evidence against Simpson was a bloody glove found at the murder scene. Tests confirmed that blood from both victims was present on the glove. In a stunning move, Simpson would later try on the glove at trial in an attempt to prove that it did not fit.

eager to bring him to trial. But Simpson was not quite ready to go to jail, and on June 17, 1994, he led police on what is undoubtedly the most bizarre and memorable police chase in history. Rather than turning himself in as agreed, Simpson disappeared with his friend Al Cowlings, who coincidentally drove a white Ford Bronco almost identical to Simpson's. As police tried to track Simpson down by tracing cellular phone calls, they were stunned by what came on the television—helicopters were filming Cowlings' Bronco. Ringed by police cars, Cowlings turned on his emergency lights and slowed down to forty miles per hour.

As people all across the nation watched the "low-speed chase" on television, Simpson held a gun to his head and threatened suicide. Cowlings pleaded with the police by telephone to let Simpson return home. As the Bronco slowly made its way toward Brentwood, more police cars joined the pursuit. Police officers spoke with Simpson on his cellular phone, begging him not to kill himself. By the time that the two men arrived at Simpson's estate, it was a circus of police and television crews. Finally, after more negotiations, Simpson surrendered. Police later found that Simpson had his passport, a fake beard, and over $8,000 with him.

With Simpson in jail as the trial approached, evidence continued to mount. The gloves were identified as an expensive pair, of which only about 300 were made; a receipt showed that Brown had purchased the very same type of gloves while she was married to Simpson. The footprints at the crime scene were the same size as Simpson's and were left by an extremely uncommon type of shoe made by Italian designer Bruno Magli; photos showed Simpson wearing these shoes.

The limousine driver created problems with Simpson's alibi—his explanation of what he was doing at the time of the murders. Although Simpson had claimed that he was at his home getting ready for his trip to Chicago when the murders occurred, the limo driver cast doubts on the story. He said that he had been trying repeatedly to call Simpson's house, but nobody answered. Meanwhile, he was driving back and forth in front of Simpson's house and had not seen Simpson's Ford Bronco. He then saw someone who looked like Simpson—in the darkness, he could not be sure—run across the driveway and into the house. After a light clicked on inside the house, the driver

called again, and this time Simpson answered.

As the case went to trial on January 24, 1995, it continued to make headlines, and networks made plans to televise all or parts of the trial. Many people around the nation were glued to their television sets as the prosecution began to introduce the evidence, which seemed to indicate Simpson's guilt very clearly. However, Simpson's lawyers had an alternative explanation: the LAPD had framed Simpson—falsified evidence to make Simpson appear guilty. They contended that Detective Fuhrman had taken the right-hand glove from the murder scene and planted it at

In a bizarre low-speed chase, police followed Simpson's white Bronco along the freeways of Los Angeles. When Simpson finally surrendered to officers, he had in his possession a fake beard, passport, and $8000 in cash.

Simpson's house. The lawyers also claimed that Detective Vannatter had taken the vial of Simpson's blood and sprinkled it on the evidence that was collected.

The defense team contended that police acted on their racism to frame Simpson, an African-American, for the murders. They discredited Fuhrman as a witness by asking him whether he used racial slurs, which he denied, and then playing recent tapes of Fuhrman using racial slurs repeatedly while talking with a Hollywood screenwriter. This tactic by Simpson's lawyers—called "playing the race card" by some—created a public furor and divided public opinion along racial lines. For many African-Americans who had experienced some form of mistreatment or disrespect from police officers, the defense struck a familiar chord. Soon, a great number of African-Americans began to believe in O.J.'s innocence—or at least to support a "not guilty" verdict in the trial.

The prosecution's case fell apart when the prosecutors asked Simpson to try on the actual gloves found at the murder scene. Simpson appeared to struggle to put them on and declared to the courtroom that they were too tight. The prosecutors tried to claim that the gloves had shrunk because they had been soaked in blood, that the latex surgical gloves that Simpson wore on his hands for protection made it more difficult to put on the gloves, and that Simpson had purposely made it more difficult to pull on the gloves by curling his fingers. But the damage was already done: members of the jury had laughed when the test failed.

On October 3, 1995, came the moment that everyone had been waiting for—the jury would announce whether or not Simpson was guilty of the murders of Brown and Goldman. Many people around the country had avidly watched the trial on television for over eight months, and everyone else who had read a newspaper, listened to the radio, or watched television in the past

After a dramatic trial in which his high-priced legal team fought to prove his innocence, O.J. Simpson was acquitted of the double murder. His family (seen here cheering amid balloons) and many others across the nation applauded the verdict, which sharply divided public opinion along racial lines.

year knew many of the details of the case. Most Americans had made up their minds already on whether or not Simpson had killed Brown and Goldman, but only the twelve people of the jury would have a say in determining Simpson's guilt.

That morning, the jury announced the verdict: not guilty. Around the country, many people celebrated, viewing the verdict as a victory against what they saw as a racist criminal justice system. At the same time, many people mourned the failure of the criminal justice system to punish someone who they believed had brutally murdered two innocent people. If O.J. was not guilty of the murders, then who was? Debates continued to rage for quite some time after the verdict was announced.

What does the O.J. Simpson trial teach us about the criminal justice system? The most important lesson is that the system does not always do a perfect job of finding out exactly what happened. In this case, the trial did not answer the question of who killed Nicole Brown and Ronald Goldman. The jury must base its decision on the evidence presented at the trial. Sometimes the prosecution is unable to present evidence—for example, if it is obtained without following proper police procedures. Also, the prosecution must prove "beyond a reasonable doubt" that a criminal defendant is guilty: "highly likely" is not good enough.

The Simpson case also shows that the justice system relies on people, and people make mistakes. In the Simpson case, the prosecutors have drawn criticism both for the failed glove fitting and for not introducing certain pieces of evidence, including any evidence about the slow-speed Bronco chase. Many have also criticized Judge Lance Ito for some of his rulings and his behavior—during the trial, he arranged for jurors to take a flight on the Goodyear blimp! In addition, the defense lawyers probably violated some rules requiring them to turn evidence over to the prosecutors and—many say—concocted a bogus story of a police frame-up to allow a guilty man to walk free. Potential witnesses were not able to testify after it was revealed that they had sold their stories to the press. The jury of twelve ordinary citizens might have misunderstood the complicated DNA evidence. Some of the other police officers made minor mistakes, and above all, Mark Fuhrman's racist views cast doubts upon the whole case.

As the 20th century ended, many people were still talking about the O.J. Simpson case, but Americans have always been fascinated by crime. In a mystery novel, the crime is solved at the end, but in real life, crime fascinates people with its unanswered questions. Sometimes the question is "Who did it?" Or "Did they have help?" Sometimes the question is "What happened?" And sometimes, the question is simply, "Why?" Some of the most famous crimes of the 20th century have left unanswered questions, even years after the trials ended.

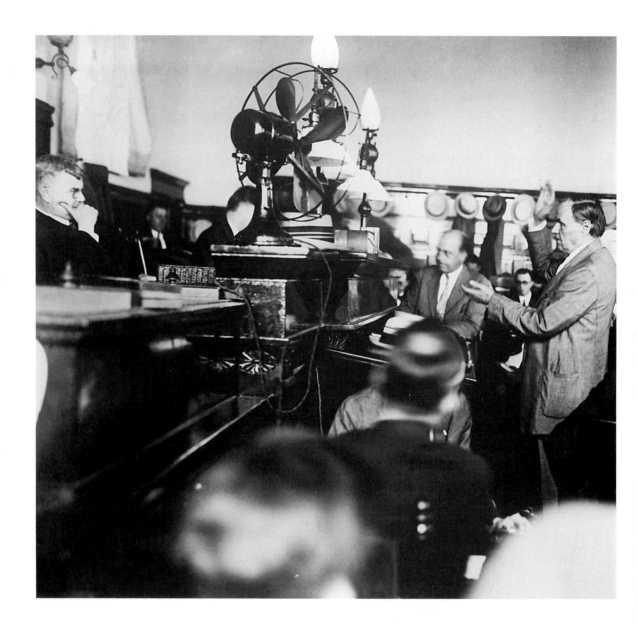

Notorious
Murder Trials
of the 1920s

Sacco & Vanzetti and Leopold & Loeb

The 1920s brought a new wave of dramatic trials to national attention. Fueled by a spirit of nationalism following World War I and the media impact of newspapers and radio, these trials made household names of many of those brought before the judge.

Throughout the 20th century, Americans have been fascinated with crimes, whether or not the suspect was a celebrity. In fact, many people accused of crimes became celebrities as newspapers, and then radio and television, made the suspects famous. During the 1920s, two notorious murder cases made headlines and captured the nation's attention, but for very different reasons.

In 1920-21, many eyes were focused on the murder case of Nicolo Sacco and Bartolomeo Vanzetti in the Boston area; the case had political overtones because the accused men were immigrants with radical anti-government views. In 1924, two young men from wealthy Chicago families, Nathan Leopold, Jr., and Richard Loeb, shocked the nation with their apparently motiveless murder of a randomly chosen teenage victim.

The cases aroused America's interests for very

different reasons. To many, the Sacco and Vanzetti trial was a gauge of the fairness of America's court system to immigrants, laborers, and the poor. By contrast, Leopold and Loeb were wealthy, intelligent young men, and people watched in fascination to see whether they would be sentenced to death; the sheer brutality and callousness of the accused men aroused America's anger.

In the early 1920s, many Americans felt a strong sense of patriotism, or love for their country, stemming from America's involvement in World War I. At the same time, a small but significant percentage of Americans were unhappy with the government, which they felt favored the wealthy more than the working class. Some of the loudest and most violent protests came from anarchists and communists. Anarchists spoke in favor of violent overthrow of the government, and some anarchist groups backed up their words with violent acts. Communists, equally mistrusted, favored a government in which working class people shared more of the power. A significant number of these unpopular anarchists and communists were people who were born in foreign countries, which led many Americans to distrust immigrants.

In an effort to protect the country from the threat of anarchists and communists, Congress passed strict laws allowing the government to deport—banish from the country—immigrants who were involved with anarchist and communist groups. The government kept a close eye on these groups through the Bureau of Investigation (which later became the FBI) and the Bureau of Immigration.

In 1920, the quiet factory town of South Braintree, Massachusetts, was the scene of a brutal murder. To this day, people debate whether the people who convicted of the crime were really responsible and whether the crime was an act of political terror or was a robbery motivated by greed. South Braintree saw very little crime of any type. But on the afternoon of April 15,

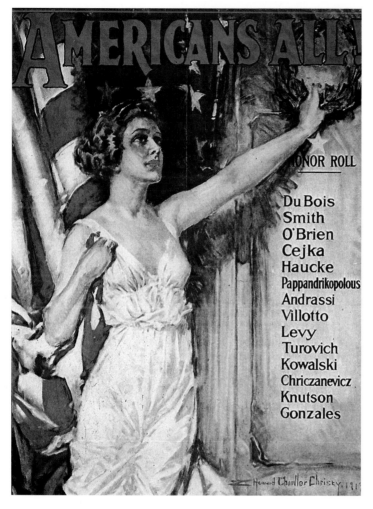

NOR ROLL

Du Bois
Smith
O'Brien
Cejka
Haucke
Pappandrikopolous
Andrassi
Villotto
Levy
Turovich
Kowalski
Chriczanevicz
Knutson
Gonzales

After World War I and the Communist revolution in Russia, a wave of nationalism and suspicion gripped America. Despite posters like this one, fear of immigrants, communists, and anarchist revolutionaries was rampant.

in broad daylight, a small group of thugs turned the town's main street into a bloody shoot-out. Although the crime shocked local residents, some would later recall seeing some suspicious activity that morning. A pale, sickly-looking man had been driving aimlessly in a dark blue car carrying four other men whom witnesses described as darker in complexion and probably Italian.

It was payday for the workers at the Slater & Morill shoe factory, and they were paid in cash. The job of distributing the pay envelopes belonged to Frederick Parmenter, who left the company's office at approximately

3:00 P.M., accompanied by his armed bodyguard, Alessandro Berardelli. The metal boxes they carried contained over $15,000 divided into envelopes.

As Parmenter and Berardelli walked down the town's main street, two men carrying handguns approached suddenly. The gunmen opened fire, killing both Parmenter and Berardelli. A third man, wielding a shotgun, jumped out of hiding. The dark blue car, with its pale driver and another man in the front seat, pulled up and disappeared with the three gunmen and the company's payroll. Berardelli's Harrington & Richardson revolver was also stolen. Because the shooting took place in broad daylight on the town's main street, a number of people saw the shooting. The gunmen also left behind several clues, including spent shells from their guns and a dark felt cap that one of the men had been wearing. Two days later the dark blue Buick used in the crime was found abandoned.

Although the crime was unusually bold, it was similar to a failed robbery attempt that had occurred in Bridgewater, Massachusetts, on December 24, 1919. On that Christmas Eve, two men with handguns and another with a shotgun attempted to rob a payroll delivery to a shoe company. The men making the delivery exchanged shots with the robbers, but nobody was hurt and the robbers escaped. Through a complicated series of events, police eventually arrested and charged two men, Nicolo Sacco and Bartolomeo Vanzetti, with the robbery and murders in Braintree, and also charged Vanzetti with the burglary in Bridgewater.

At the time, the federal government was actively deporting foreign anarchists. By coincidence, on the day after the South Braintree murders, police went to visit Italian immigrant Feruccio Coacci at his home in Cochessett, Massachusetts, because he had missed a deportation hearing scheduled for the previous day. Coacci, who previously had been challenging his deportation, suddenly seemed eager to return to Italy.

He had used his wife's illness as an excuse for missing the hearing, but she did not appear ill to the police. However, because Coacci was cooperative in wanting to return to Italy, the police officers simply gave him a ride so that he could catch a boat to his homeland.

Since the Christmas Eve robbery attempt, Bridgewater's police chief Michael Stewart had been looking for suspects. When Stewart learned of the Braintree murders and realized that Coacci had missed his deportation hearing on that same day, he became suspicious. By then, Coacci had already departed for Italy, so Stewart visited Coacci's former residence looking for clues. Another Italian man, Mike Boda, greeted Chief Stewart and another officer at the door. Boda allowed the officers to look around, and the police chief was especially interested to discover tire tracks at the residence. Because witnesses had described the Bridgeport robbers as Italian and the getaway car was headed toward Cochessett, Chief Stewart had been looking for Italian men who drove cars in Cochessett.

Boda told Stewart that he owned an Overland (a relatively small car) that was being repaired at the nearby Elm Street Garage. However, Stewart noticed a second set of tire tracks that belong to a much larger car, which he suspected might have been the Buick used in the Braintree robbery. Although Stewart did not arrest or interrogate Boda at the time, he returned in a few days, only to find the residence abandoned. Hoping to track down Boda through his car, he then told the owner of the Elm Street Garage to call him when Boda came to pick up the car.

Boda did not attempt to retrieve his car from the Elm Street Garage for some time. One evening Boda arrived past closing time with three other men, and the garage owner contacted the police. Suspecting something was wrong, Boda and his friends left. Boda rode in the sidecar of a motorcycle driven by one of the men, and the two others left on foot and boarded a streetcar.

Nicolo Sacco (right) and Bartolomeo Vanzetti (center) were two Italian anarchists whose openly anti-American views worked against them. Arrested for murder and robbery committed in two Massachusetts towns, both were convicted and sentenced to death.

When Chief Stewart arrived at the garage, the men were already gone. He called the police in nearby Brockton and asked them to arrest two foreign-looking men on the streetcar. The Brockton police arrested Sacco and Vanzetti; both carried handguns, and Vanzetti was also carrying anarchist literature. Boda, meanwhile, fled to Italy.

In much the same way that the police arrested Sacco and Vanzetti through a strange turn of events, prosecutors brought the two men to trial using confusing and contradictory evidence. The men's lawyer, Fred Moore, publicly claimed that that they were being framed for the murders because they were foreign and because of their anti-government views. He succeeded in arousing widespread interest in the case, both in the United

States and Europe. Many laborers, immigrants, and intellectuals supported Sacco and Vanzetti's cause.

The trial itself did little to calm the anger of people who thought that the two men were being framed. The eyewitness evidence was contradictory. The prosecutors called numerous witnesses who claimed to have seen Sacco and Vanzetti at the scene of the murder. However, the defense presented various witnesses who claimed to have seen Sacco at a Boston restaurant and to have seen Vanzetti selling fish in Plymouth at the time of the murders. Vanzetti, in a letter to Alvan Fuller, the governor of Massachusetts, would later point out that the conflicting testimony allowed the jury to act upon their own prejudices:

> People don't seem to understand that Italians are unpopular any way, especially if they are poor and laboring people . . . They don't get the same chance before an American jury that an American would get. The jury cannot help being prejudiced against them, and then if on top of that the Italians turn out to be Radicals, they have no [chance] at all. One good looking American witness seems to outweigh a dozen Italian witnesses . . .

Apart from the eyewitness testimony, the case against Vanzetti hinged on the fact that he had been arrested while carrying a Harrington & Richardson revolver similar to the one taken from Berardelli during the murders. The prosecution highlighted Vanzetti's inconsistent stories about how he had gotten the gun and why he had it. In his letter to Governor Fuller, Vanzetti claimed that—not knowing that he was a suspect in the Bridgewater and Braintree crimes—he had lied to police to protect his radical friends from being caught with guns or communist literature. The "lies that I have said have no relation whatever with the crimes," he wrote. Years later, it would be revealed that the prosecution knew that the serial number of Berardelli's gun was different from that of Vanzetti's gun; in fact, there was a good chance that

Berardelli's gun used different size bullets (.32 caliber) from the one carried by Vanzetti (.38 caliber).

There was somewhat more evidence against Sacco, who had missed work at another shoe factory on the day of the murders. The factory owner's son testified that the felt cap found at the murder scene was similar in color and style to one that Sacco frequently wore to work. More importantly, the prosecution called a witness, Captain William H. Proctor, of the Massachusetts State Police, who was an expert in ballistics—the science of matching bullets to the guns that fired them. When asked whether the Colt automatic that was taken from Sacco during his arrest had fired one of the bullets that killed Berardelli, Proctor replied, "My opinion is that it is consistent with having been fired from that pistol." He did not say that it had definitely been fired by Sacco's gun, and in the decades following the trial, the ballistics evidence would be a subject of continuing controversy.

Despite the questionable evidence, the prosecution closed its case with a plea to the jurors that they must convict Sacco and Vanzetti in order to uphold justice. Judge Webster Thayer seemed to echo the sentiments of the prosecution. On the afternoon of July 14, 1921, the case went to the jury, and by 7:30 that evening, the jury had reached its verdict: guilty. Sacco's wife shrieked, and Sacco shouted angrily that the court would kill two innocent men.

After the guilty verdict, the men's lawyers tried repeatedly to appeal the verdict—to overturn the conviction or earn a new trial. Harvard law professor Felix Frankfurter, who would later become a U.S. Supreme Court Justice, publicly took up the cause of Sacco and Vanzetti. He even wrote a book in which he exposed Captain Proctor's testimony as given "by prearrangement with the District Attorney" and stated that, had one of the attorneys asked Proctor whether he could be sure that the bullet came from Sacco's gun, "he would, as he

Despite the efforts of defense attorneys and many public protests on their behalf, Sacco and Vanzetti were executed in 1927. Their death masks are seen here on display at Boston Public Library in 1999.

says, have been obliged to answer in the negative . . ."

Although the appeals process lasted several years, none of the attorneys' efforts were successful in overturning the guilty verdict. On April 9, 1927, after listening to Sacco and Vanzetti once again proclaim their innocence, Judge Thayer sentenced each of the men to die in the electric chair. As August 10, 1927—the date of the planned execution—approached, there was unrest around the world. In major cities across the United States, labor strikes and street demonstrations protested the impending execution. In Europe, Australia, and South America, there were protests near U.S. embassies. Major newspapers denounced the verdict and the death sentence. But that night, Sacco and Vanzetti went to the electric chair. Vanzetti died proclaiming his innocence; Sacco shouted "Long live anarchy!"

Many historians and scholars agree that Sacco and Vanzetti did not receive a fair trial, due in large part to the prejudices of judge and jury against immigrants and political radicals. In the decades after the trial, public and scholarly opinion seemed to accept Sacco and Vanzetti's innocence. However, evidence uncovered later suggests that one of the men might have indeed been guilty.

Four decades after the trial, new ballistics tests indicated that a fatal bullet was indeed fired from Sacco's gun. Adding to the speculation, the son of the man who led Sacco and Vanzetti's anarchist group claimed that everyone in the group "knew that Sacco was guilty and that Vanzetti was innocent as far as the actual participation in the killing. But no one would ever break the code of silence even if it cost Vanzetti's life." Perhaps by refusing to testify against any of his fellow anarchists, Vanzetti went to the electric chair for them.

Most people continue to believe that both Sacco and Vanzetti were innocent. Some have suggested that the bullet that later proved to have been fired from Sacco's gun was actually planted by the prosecutors to help strengthen their case. In 1977, on the fiftieth anniversary of Sacco and Vanzetti's execution, Massachusetts Governor Michael Dukakis declared the day to be "Nicolo Sacco and Bartolomeo Vanzetti Memorial Day," stating: "The atmosphere of their trial and appeals was permeated by prejudice against foreigners and hostility toward unorthodox political views . . ." Although Dukakis did not reverse the verdict, he pronounced it to be a product of trouble times.

In addition to being a time of political unrest for the working class, the 1920s were also the "Roaring Twenties" for the middle and upper classes, characterized by newfound wealth, jazz music, shorter dresses, and wild parties. While Sacco and Vanzetti were poor immigrants bound by their loyalty to anarchist groups, Nathan Leopold, Jr., and Richard Loeb shared a different kind of bond:

> Both were wealthy; both lived in imposing houses in the same neighborhood on the South Side of Chicago. They drove expensive cars. They drank. They smoked. They had been graduated from college at an age when most boys were being graduated from high school.

In 1924 Nathan Leopold, Jr., was a law student at the University of Chicago and hoped to attend Harvard University the next academic year. He was also deeply interested in philosophy, and he was considered a national expert on birds; at nineteen, he was considered to be the nation's leading expert on a particular type of songbird. His father was a wealthy industrialist.

Richard Loeb was also wealthy, the son of a vice president of Sears, Roebuck & Company. Though only eighteen, he had graduated a year earlier from the University of Michigan and was extremely intelligent. He was also charming, as his partner-in-crime Leopold recalls, "Everybody went for the guy—and rightly so. There wasn't a sunnier, pleasanter, more likable fellow in the world."

Despite all of their advantages and talent, what linked Leopold and Loeb together in history was that they shared a morbid desire to commit a perfect crime. In the months leading up to May 1924, they allegedly committed a number of crimes such as break-ins while they carefully planned their biggest crime—kidnapping for ransom. The two discussed how to carry out each element of the crime to avoid detection: kidnapping the victim, notifying the victim's family, collecting the ransom, etc. They decided that, in order to avoid identification by their victim, they would not only have

Another case that captured national attention was that of Nathan Leopold (right) and Richard Loeb (left). Both were intellectually gifted sons of wealthy families. Leopold and Loeb were tried and convicted in a bizarre kidnapping and murder plot.

to kidnap him, but also have to murder him.

On May 21, 1924, the young men cruised through their own neighborhood looking for a victim. They drove a rental car to avoid being seen in one of their own cars. At approximately 5:00 P.M., they lured fourteen-year old Bobby Franks into the car. The unsuspecting victim was killed with a chisel, and the two murderers hid his body in the end of an open drainage pipe in a park known to Leopold through his bird-watching.

Leopold and Loeb then moved on to the second phase of their crime: collecting the ransom money from

Franks' wealthy father. Communicating by telephone and special delivery letter, the murderers assured Jacob Franks that his son was still alive, and that Bobby would be returned unharmed if the elder Franks paid a $10,000 ransom. The two men gave Franks instructions to throw the ransom money from a train at a particular spot. However, before the two could collect the ransom, their "perfect" crime began to unravel. Despite their superior intelligence and extensive planning, the two young criminals had made some mistakes. As they went to collect the ransom, they stopped to get a newspaper. Before they even picked up the paper, they saw the headline: "BODY OF BOY FOUND IN SWAMP."

They had not counted on Franks' body being discovered before they collected the ransom—Mr. Franks would surely not pay the ransom if he knew that his son was dead. However, the two held out hope that Mr. Franks had not yet gotten the news. When the train chugged past and no money appeared, the two realized that they would never get the ransom. They were disappointed but remained confident that they would not be caught. They did not realize that they had made another mistake: they had left behind a clue that would lead the police directly to Leopold.

When the two murderers disposed of Franks' body in the drainage pipe in the park, Leopold dropped a pair of reading glasses. Because he rarely used these glasses, he had no idea that he had left them at the scene of the crime. In fact, he was quite surprised when police first questioned him about the murder. He told the police that he must have lost his glasses while bird-watching. He gave them the alibi that Loeb and he had rehearsed—that the two had taken Leopold's car to a park to pick up some girls. It was only through a stroke of great luck that police were able to track the glasses to Leopold. The glasses used an extremely unusual type of hinge, and the one eye doctor in

Leopold and Loeb's plan to commit "the perfect crime" unraveled when police discovered the body of their victim, 13-year-old Robert Franks. Despite the efforts of renowned lawyer Clarence Darrow, evidence eventually led to their conviction. Loeb later died in prison, while Leopold was paroled in 1958, after serving more than 30 years.

Chicago who prescribed glasses with this hinge led investigators to Leopold, one of only a handful of patients for whom he had done so.

The police gathered other evidence. They determined that the typewriter used for the ransom note had been taken from Leopold's law school. Also, the Leopold family's chauffeur told investigators that Leopold's car had not left the garage on the day of the murder, thereby discrediting the two men's alibi. Faced with strong evidence, each of the men confessed. During Loeb's confession, he told the State's Attorney that, in planning the murder, the two had selected "[n]obody in particular" and that they had chosen Franks "by pure accident." This random act of violence shocked the public.

Also shocking was the callousness of the two murderers. Leopold recalls: "[I]t was all a game to [Loeb]. He reminded me of an eight-year-old all wrapped up in a game of cops and robbers." Leopold admits that he, too, was able to commit the crime without any feelings of remorse at the time:

> It was a busy time for me, that week. One of my brothers had just announced his engagement. There was a dinner party every night at the home of one or another friend or relative. And there was only another ten days of school. Final examinations in all five of my law courses. And then there were the Harvard exams I had to take in the meantime.
>
> Today it seems incredible that I could have taken part in my everyday activities, could have lived a normal-appearing life, with the dread knowledge of what I had done on my conscience.

With the threat of the death penalty very real, the families hired defense lawyers including Clarence Darrow, one of the most famous lawyers of the century. Darrow tried an innovative strategy to try to save the lives of Leopold and Loeb. If the defendants pled "not guilty by reason of insanity," they would have faced a jury, and Darrow feared that the jury would have convicted the two and sentenced them to death. Instead, Darrow counseled his two clients to plead guilty. His strategy was to claim not that the men were legally insane—unable to tell right from wrong—but that the two men were mentally ill and therefore deserving of the judge's mercy.

Having pled guilty, Leopold and Loeb faced not a trial, but a sentencing hearing, in which Judge John Caverly would decide whether to sentence each defendant to fourteen or more years in prison, life in person, or death by execution. During the hearing, which lasted over a month, the defense presented people who knew the defendants, as well as several prominent psychiatrists. State's Attorney Crowe presented his own expert witnesses who claimed that the defendants were not mentally ill, and Crowe also painstakingly put on a case to prove the crime, in an effort to remind Judge Caverly of the brutality of Leopold and Loeb's actions. Darrow ended the hearing with a passionate plea to Judge Caverly. He pled for the court's understanding and mercy. He argued that the death penalty was cruel and would not solve the problems created by Leopold and Loeb's actions. Some in the courtroom, including Leopold, were in tears after the moving speech.

Two weeks later, Leopold and Loeb returned to Judge Caverly's courtroom to learn their sentence. The courtroom was packed with both curious onlookers and reporters from every major newspaper in America. Several times, Leopold and Loeb thought that they would hang. Judge Caverly announced that the guilty plea would not influence his decision because the state's attorney had proven the crime. He also said that the psychiatric testimony would have no impact. However, the judge finally revealed the sentence—life in prison, plus 99 years—saying that the defendants' young age made him unwilling to sentence them to death.

Despite having his life spared by the judge, Richard Loeb would meet an untimely death while in prison. On January 28, 1936, Nathan Leopold, Jr., learned that his friend was in the prison hospital after an attack by another inmate. Leopold begged to be let in. Loeb lay on an operating table, his throat slashed and bleeding profusely. Leopold was not able to say goodbye to his friend, who died without regaining consciousness.

Leopold himself fared better. He tried to be a model prisoner, teaching classes and working in the prison hospital. While in prison, he wrote a book about the case, *Life Plus 99 Years*, in which he did not provide any specific details of the murder itself. When Leopold was paroled from prison in 1958, public interest in his case remained strong, and he left Illinois forever for a quiet existence in Puerto Rico. But like Sacco and Vanzetti, history has not forgotten Leopold and Loeb.

THE GANGSTERS
AND G-MEN
OF THE 1930s

*The Crime Wave of 1932-34
and the Rise of the FBI*

The 1920s and 1930s saw the rise of a new type of American criminal —the gangster. Tommy guns and daring daylight bank robberies increased during the Great Depression. Among the FBI's most wanted in 1934 were (clockwise from top left) John Dillinger, Arthur Barker, "Pretty Boy" Floyd, Homer Van Meter, Alvin Karpis, and "Baby Face" Nelson.

The early 1930s were a time of economic desperation known as the "Great Depression." It started with the stock market "crash" of October 29, 1929. Many people who had invested their money in companies' stock—shares of ownership—lost their savings as investors panicked and sold off stock for a fraction of what they had paid. As company after company failed, millions lost their jobs: in some cities, four out of every five people were unemployed. Many banks also failed, unable to repay the people who had deposited their money. People did whatever they could just to survive and feed their families. Because the sale or possession of alcohol was illegal during the "Prohibition" era of 1919-1933, many people turned to "bootlegging," or selling illegal liquor, as a way to make money.

Against this backdrop of desperate times, a new breed of criminal emerged: the serial bank robber. During the years of 1932 through 1934, a crime wave swept the nation: gangs of bank robbers roamed from big city to big city, and small town to small town. The gangs were usually one step ahead of the law, but when the law caught up with them, the gangsters often escaped through a bloody shoot-out. Even when the law captured them alive, the gangsters often escaped from prison, alone or with the help of other criminals.

The gangsters were able to pull off increasingly daring heists and continue to elude police by arming themselves with powerful new weapons. In addition to shotguns and high-powered hunting rifles, the gangsters found a faithful friend in the Thompson submachine gun. Called a submachine gun because it fires pistol shells rather than rifle shells, the "Tommy gun" was light enough to carry on bank jobs, but could keep the police at bay with a rapid spray of bullets.

Between heists, the gangsters hid out with the assistance of friends, family, and fellow criminals. And surprisingly, the gangsters often received help from ordinary citizens. Prohibition had given many people a disdain for the government, and in the desperate times of the Great Depression, people often viewed bank robbers as heroes, or at least as "Robin Hoods" who victimized only the wealthy. Even the killings of lawmen were overlooked to some extent, as many considered sheriffs and police officers to be lackeys of the banks who evicted people from their homes.

Certain gangsters captured the nation's fascination through their personal charisma. Fueled by newsreels shown at movie theaters and crime magazines detailing gangsters' exploits, the popularity of gangsters such as Charles "Pretty Boy" Floyd, Bonnie Parker and Clyde Barrow, and John Dillinger grew. During the gangsters' heyday of 1932-34, all over an obsessed nation, people reported seeing the infamous criminals.

Although police forces were certainly not happy with the gangsters' exploits, they contributed to the gangsters' legendary status by blaming almost any unsolved crime on a high-profile criminal. Bonnie Parker, who wrote poetry when not committing crimes, recorded her sentiments in "The Story of Bonnie and Clyde":

> If a policeman is killed in Dallas
> And they have no clue or guide
> If they can't find a fiend, just wipe the slate clean
> And hang it on Bonnie and Clyde.

Floyd, Parker, Barrow, and Dillinger had much in common besides their charm and their crimes. They used time behind bars to their advantage by learning from fellow convicts how to commit crimes. When cornered, they shot to kill, and when captured, they escaped, but ultimately, they all died in ambushes by law enforcement officials.

Charles Arthur "Pretty Boy" Floyd grew up in Eastern Oklahoma idolizing the outlaws of the "Old West," such as Jesse James. However, Floyd's career as a bandit got off to a rough start. In 1925, he was sentenced to five years in prison for his role in a grocery store payroll robbery in St. Louis, Missouri. But it was inside the Missouri State Penitentiary that his criminal career really began. Floyd entered the "state pen" as an inexperienced petty criminal, caught in his first attempt at a major crime. When he was paroled in 1929, an assortment of hardened criminals had given him training in cracking safes, driving getaway cars, hiding from the police, and other criminal techniques. He was ready to become a career criminal.

Following advice from fellow convicts, Floyd moved to Kansas City, Missouri, where his good looks earned him the nickname "Pretty Boy," which he hated. While in Kansas City, he reunited with ex-convicts he knew from the Missouri State Penitentiary and also met other criminals. In late 1929, Floyd and two friends left Kansas City looking for banks to rob.

Floyd's first bank robbery was not a memorable one. When Floyd and his accomplices stormed into a bank in Sylvania, Ohio, with guns drawn, a cashier alertly closed

Charles Arthur "Pretty Boy" Floyd grew up in Oklahoma, idolizing western outlaws like Jesse James. Educated in the ways of crime while in prison, Floyd went on to become one of America's most notorious bank robbers.

the vault, which was equipped with a time lock that would not allow the vault to be opened for several hours. Frustrated, the robbers grabbed whatever cash they could from the tellers' drawers. An eyewitness across the street called the telephone operator, who alerted the fire department, the sheriff, and the police in nearby Toledo. The sound of the sirens scared off the robbers, but only the fire department had responded. For a time, the fire chief pursued the getaway car in his fire truck, but the gang escaped to their hideout in Akron, Ohio. Their freedom would be short-lived: Akron police soon arrested Floyd and his accomplices. Faced with overwhelming evidence, Floyd pled guilty, but he had not given up.

On December 10, 1930, as a prison train transferred a group of convicts from the Toledo jail to the Ohio State Penitentiary in Columbus, Floyd made a daring escape. He managed to break the chains that bound him to another prisoner and jump out a window into the dark night. Rather than running, he hid among some tall weeds and somehow managed to remain undetected until the searchers gave up. He would never again be "taken alive" by police.

Floyd returned to Kansas City long enough to hook up with a new partner in crime, Willis "Billy the Killer" Miller. They were involved in illegal activities, including bootlegging. However, the two soon became suspects in the murder of two brothers, themselves petty criminals. Floyd and Miller left Kansas City with two sisters—who just so happened to have been romantically involved with the slain brothers. Floyd and Miller reportedly robbed several banks together before police caught up with them. On April 16, 1931, police in Bowling Green, Ohio, attempted to apprehend Floyd and Miller. In the ensuing shoot-out, Floyd made it out alive, but Miller did not.

Floyd eventually found another steady partner in George Birdwell. The pair robbed a number of Oklahoma banks in 1931 and 1932. They never wore masks and had a signature style:

> Wielding submachine guns and revolvers, steel chest protectors under their expensive suits, shoes spit-shined, Floyd and company struck in broad daylight just as the old-time bandit heroes had done. Floyd joked and chatted with bank employees and avoided strong-armed force; the image was as important as the take.

After looting a bank, they would drive away, forcing several bank employees to stand on the getaway car's running boards—platforms that extended outside the doors of cars built in that era. Shielded by hostages, Floyd and Birdwell knew that nobody would shoot at them.

In April 1932, Floyd killed a retired sheriff who had set a trap for him, hoping to collect several thousand dollars in reward money. (This was the only killing to which Floyd would ever admit.) Oklahoma authorities intensified the manhunt, but despite growing posses and help from pioneer aviator Wiley Post, Oklahoma authorities could not catch Pretty Boy Floyd. Boldly making regular visits to family members around the state, he became a true Oklahoma folk hero, with rumors circulating that he bought meals and gave money to poor farmers. It was widely believed that when he robbed banks, he tore up mortgages—the documents that allowed banks to take over farms and homes if loans were not repaid. It is difficult to distinguish fact from legend, but law enforcement officials constantly complained that the people of Oklahoma helped to hide Floyd from authorities.

On November 1, 1932, Floyd proved to the nation what a popular figure he had become. During the noon hour, Floyd and Birdwell strolled into a bank in their usual way. But this was no ordinary bank—it was the bank in Floyd's hometown of Sallisaw, Oklahoma. On his way into the bank, he paused to speak to people in the street and in the barbershop next door. While Floyd and Birdwell robbed the bank, police chief Bert Cotton was only 75 feet from the bank, but he denied knowing that anything was going on.

However, Floyd's luck was beginning to run out. Only three weeks after the Sallisaw robbery, Birdwell attempted his first bank robbery without Floyd and was gunned down by a bank employee. Although Floyd found a new partner, Adam Richetti, and continued to rob banks, a fateful event on June 17, 1933, made Pretty Boy the subject of a national manhunt coordinated by the FBI. On that day, law enforcement officials were returning fugitive Frank Nash to Missouri to stand trial. The Agents transported Nash by train to Kansas City. Then, according to FBI files: "occurred in front of the Union Railway Station in Kansas City, Missouri one of the most brutal, premeditated mass murders recorded in the annals of American law enforcement. The killings . . . are now known as 'The Kansas City Massacre.'"

As Nash was being loaded into a waiting police car, three men approached, machine guns blazing. They gunned down an Oklahoma police chief, two Kansas City policemen, an FBI agent, as well as Nash. The head of the FBI's Kansas City office and another agent were wounded. The gunmen made a clean getaway, but back east in Washington, D.C., FBI director J. Edgar Hoover eventually put the finger for the Kansas City Massacre on Pretty Boy:

> Immediately following this daring crime which shocked the nation, the FBI instituted an intensive investigation to identify and apprehend these maddened gunmen. Following months of painstaking work, with all of the facilities at its disposal, the FBI uncovered positive evidence that this scheme was executed by Vernon C. Miller, Adam C. Richetti, and Charles Arthur Floyd . . .

Floyd denied involvement in the Kansas City Massacre, and many who knew Floyd supported his claims. Some historians believe that the massacre was out of character

Despite his denials, "Pretty Boy" Floyd was targeted by the FBI as the one responsible for the Kansas City Massacre of 1933, which resulted in the deaths of an Oklahoma police chief, two Kansas City officers, an FBI agent, and fugitive Frank Nash.

for Floyd, who previously had only shot when cornered. Regardless of whether he participated, the FBI had settled on Floyd as its prime suspect, and he went into hiding as long as he could—until the FBI would start to catch up with the gangsters.

While Floyd's bank robbing career was already well underway, another pair of gangsters began to share the spotlight. Bonnie Parker and Clyde Barrow captured national headlines not only with their brutal crime spree, but also because their love affair made an interesting story for the newspapers. When Bonnie Parker met Clyde Barrow in January 1930, he already a veteran of several bank robberies. As Clyde's sister Marie recalls: "Apparently, it was love at first sight for both of them, and each seemed to find a meaningful and truly close relationship with each other." It must have been love at first sight for Bonnie, because she didn't have long to make up her mind: when she brought Clyde home to meet her mother in Dallas, Texas, police officers also met up with Clyde and arrested him on robbery charges.

With her new love in jail, Bonnie—who had previously not been in any serious trouble—made a fateful decision. In March, Bonnie smuggled a revolver to Clyde in the Waco, Texas, jail where he was being held. Although Bonnie returned to Dallas and waited anxiously for him to return, Clyde and two other escapees instead committed a string of robberies and car thefts. However, they were soon recaptured and returned to the Waco jail.

Barrow was sentenced to fourteen years in prison, and was later assigned to the nearby Eastham State Prison Farm to do hard labor. Clyde was desperate to get out; in fact, according to fellow inmate Ralph Fults, Clyde vowed that one day he would get out, form a gang, and return to shoot the guards and free the prisoners. However, he developed a less violent, but nonetheless painful plan: he staged an "accident" in which another inmate cut off two of Barrow's toes with an axe. The ruse worked, and Barrow was paroled in February 1932.

Soon, Bonnie and Clyde would not only reunite as lovers, but also form one of the most memorable criminal duos in history. During 1932 and 1933, working with gang members that included Clyde's brother Buck, Raymond Hamilton, and W.D. "Deacon" Jones, Bonnie and Clyde robbed banks, general stores, and company payrolls. During one robbery, Hamilton killed a storeowner, allegedly by accident.

Although Hamilton was captured, tried, and convicted for murder, Bonnie and Clyde remained on the run, sometimes relying on Clyde's skill as a getaway driver, and sometimes shooting their way out of ambushes. In 1933, the Barrow gang had rented a house in Joplin, Missouri, which had a reputation as a safe haven for gangsters. However, local police decided to raid the house—a decision that proved fatal. On April 13, the gang exchanged gunfire with local police and Missouri state troopers, but Bonnie and Clyde, together with Jones, Buck, and Buck's wife, Blanche, all escaped. With two lawmen dead and two others injured, the authorities were left with nothing except a few rolls of film. While the film did not prove valuable in tracking the gang, newspapers delighted in publishing the photos, especially one of Bonnie holding a revolver in her hand and a cigar in her mouth.

Through the end of 1933, Bonnie and Clyde continued to make headlines with robberies, kidnappings, and shootouts. They even raided a National Guard armory in Enid, Oklahoma, to get more weapons and ammunition. However, the law was taking its toll on the gang. On July 29, Buck Barrow was killed and Blanche was arrested during a police shootout in Iowa. In November, "Deacon" Jones was captured in Houston. However, Bonnie and Clyde made it through to the New Year still on the run.

It was in early 1934 that Bonnie and Clyde pulled their most daring caper, the one that ultimately led to their doom. With former gang member Raymond Hamilton locked up in Eastham State Prison Farm—the same facility in which Clyde had served time, and which he had vowed

Perhaps the most famous criminal duo of the 1930s was that of Bonnie Parker and Clyde Barrow. Together, Bonnie and Clyde robbed a series of banks, general stores, and company payrolls before being ambushed and killed by law enforcement officers in 1934.

to raid one day—the gang began to plot with Hamilton's family to spring the convicted murderer. In preparation, guns were smuggled to Hamilton and another inmate, Joe Palmer. On the foggy morning of January 16, Clyde and one of Hamilton's friends, James Mullen, hid near where the prisoners would be cutting timber. When the prisoners arrived at the edge of the woods, Hamilton and Palmer opened fire, killing one of the guards. Clyde fired a machine gun to provide cover as Hamilton, Palmer, and three other convicts rushed to the car where Bonnie waited with the engine running. Although no plans had been made for the three additional men, Bonnie and Clyde herded everyone into the car.

Hamilton and another of the escapees, Henry Methvin, would soon join with Bonnie and Clyde to rob more banks. But the state of Texas had had enough of Bonnie and Clyde, and on February 1, the governor met with former Texas Ranger Frank Hamer to talk him into coming out of retirement. Hamer agreed and began the hunt, along with the FBI.

The FBI, meanwhile, had other concerns. In addition to "Pretty Boy" Floyd and Bonnie and Clyde, the FBI was in search of the nation's first "Public Enemy Number One," John Dillinger. In just 14 months, Dillinger pulled off one of the most famous crime sprees in the nation's history. Like Pretty Boy Floyd, John Dillinger was sentenced to prison after bungling a robbery as a youth. And as Floyd had done, Dillinger used his 8½ years in prison to learn the tricks of the trade. He left the Indiana State Prison on May 22, 1933, with new ideas, as well as a list of businesses to rob and potential gang members. In his first four months out of prison, he allegedly participated in at least ten robberies. During this time, he developed one of his trademarks—athletically vaulting over bank counters to collect the money.

When he was arrested for bank robbery on September 22, exactly four months after being released from prison, it appeared that Dillinger was destined to spend a lot more time behind bars. However, that was not to be the case. A few days later, while Dillinger was in the Lima, Ohio, jail awaiting trial, eight men escaped from the Indiana State Prison. (It was later discovered that before Dillinger was arrested, he had aided the escape by throwing guns over the prison wall.)

On October 12, four of the escapees—Harry Pierpont, Charles Makley, John Hamilton, and Russell Clark— arrived at the Lima jail to return the favor. Accompanying

John Dillinger was a true icon of American crime in the 1930s. He was known not only for his daring bank robberies, but also for his brazen claim that no prison built could hold him. In fact, Dillinger did escape from custody twice—in Ohio and Indiana—before being gunned down by FBI agent Melvin Purvis outside Chicago's Biograph Theatre.

them was Harry Copeland, another of Dillinger's accomplices. After failing to convince the sheriff's deputy that they were picking up Dillinger for a parole violation, the men opened fire, killing the deputy. For the time being, John Dillinger was free again, and the five men who helped him to escape would form the nucleus of his gang. Dillinger did not want to waste any time in resuming his career as a bank robber, but to do it right, he would need the proper weaponry. Working with two of his gang members, he robbed two Indiana police stations for bulletproof vests, machine guns, rifles, handguns, and ammunition. With heavily armed criminals on the loose, Governor Paul McNutt called up the National Guard to assist in the manhunt.

Undeterred by the attention, Dillinger and his gang

pulled off a series of bank robberies in several states. However, the heat on the gang increased when Dillinger allegedly killed an Indiana police officer on January 15, 1934. The gang decided to lay low for a while in Tucson, Arizona, feeling that that they would be safe in the warm weather vacation spot, far away from their pursuers. They were wrong: on January 25, Tucson police arrested Dillinger, Pierpont, Makley, and Clark. Several states fought for the right to put the men on trial, but it was decided that Dillinger would go to Indiana to face charges including murdering the policeman, and the others would go to Ohio to face charges of murdering the sheriff's deputy during the Lima jailbreak.

On January 30, Dillinger was transferred to the Lake County Jail in Indiana. By then, Dillinger was a national celebrity, and the local prosecutor posed for a chummy picture with Dillinger in the jail, which officials bragged was "inescapable." After spending just over a month behind bars, Dillinger proved them wrong. On March 3, Dillinger somehow used a wooden gun to escape. Adding insult to injury, he stole the sheriff's car and escaped to Illinois. Almost immediately, Dillinger teamed up with veteran gangsters Homer Van Meter and "Baby Face Nelson" (Lester Gillis) and began robbing banks again. Compared to everything else Dillinger had done, stealing the car seemed minor. But when Dillinger drove the car across state lines, he broke a federal law for the first time, which meant that the FBI could begin to pursue Dillinger.

In April 1934, Pretty Boy Floyd, Bonnie and Clyde, and John Dillinger were all at large. It was a disaster: although banks were losing money and lawmen were losing their lives, the public still seemed to root for the gangsters. In Washington, D.C., Attorney General Homer Cummings, the nation's top prosecutor; President Franklin Roosevelt; and Congress worked together to strengthen the power of federal agents, with greater resources and greater authority. In its efforts to stop the gangsters, the FBI made vast improvements in its crime fighting ability. It started a centralized database of fingerprints and criminal records and began to send information across the country with teletype machines, an early version of today's fax machine.

Top law enforcement officials also realized that to stop the gangsters' crimes, they would also have to turn the public against the gangsters. J. Edgar Hoover began a publicity campaign to make his FBI agents—not the gangsters—national heroes. He popularized the term "G-men" (government men) to refer to his agents, claiming that the term originated with the capture of kidnapper George "Machine Gun" Kelly, who—the bureau claimed—pleaded, "Don't shoot, G-men!" when he was captured.

On April 23, 1934, the FBI closed in on Dillinger, Van Meter, and Baby Face. Acting on a tip from the owners of the rural Little Bohemia resort in northern Wisconsin, FBI agents from St. Paul and Chicago flew to the nearest airport, 50 miles away. Under the leadership of Melvin Purvis, the head of the FBI's Chicago office, the agents surrounded the resort. Seeing three men exit a building, the agents called for them to stop, but the men got into the car and started to drive away. Reacting quickly, the agents opened fire, but unfortunately, they had the wrong men. The three were innocent citizens who were frightened by the shouting and did not realize that the men yelling at them were federal agents. One of the men was killed, and the other two were injured.

When the gangsters heard the gunshots, they returned fire with machine guns and then began to flee. Dillinger and Van Meter got away cleanly. In a neighboring resort, Baby Face met up with two FBI agents and a local police constable. He opened fire on the officers, killing one FBI agent and wounding the constable, then escaped in the constable's car. When the FBI agents finally stormed the Little Bohemia, all of the gangsters had escaped, but they arrested three women who had been with the gangsters,

A well-planned ambush by Texas Ranger Frank Hamer (seen here) and five deputies ended the criminal careers of Bonnie and Clyde in a hail of gunfire on a Louisiana road. The deaths of these two outlaws helped intensify efforts by J. Edgar Hoover and the FBI to capture those who remained at large.

including Baby Face's wife. The raid was a disaster, and many people called for Purvis and Hoover to resign.

However, the gangsters' luck was finally running out. On May 23, 1934, the retired Texas Ranger Frank Hamer finally caught up with Bonnie and Clyde. He and five other men set an ambush for the pair, and as the gangsters drove down a rural Louisiana road, the posse riddled the car with bullets from their high-powered rifles. Bonnie and Clyde's death made national headlines, and the "death car" became a tourist attraction.

Although the FBI was not involved in the ambush in Louisiana, its agents gained some hope that the other gangsters could eventually be stopped. As Hoover's

FBI Agent Melvin Purvis (left), the man responsible for bringing down "Public Enemy Number One," John Dillinger, is congratulated by Attorney General William Stanley (center), and FBI Director J. Edgar Hoover (right). Years later, Purvis committed suicide with the same gun used to kill Dillinger.

publicity campaign intensified, public sentiment began to turn against the gangsters. And as rewards increased, it became more and more difficult for the gangsters to find places to hide. On June 23, Dillinger became the nation's first "Public Enemy Number One."

Eager for a chance to redeem himself for the disaster at Little Bohemia, Melvin Purvis doggedly pursued Dillinger and his gang. In late July, Purvis got the lead that he needed. A woman who knew Dillinger reported that he would be at the Biograph Theatre in Chicago on the afternoon of July 22. As Dillinger left the movie theater, Purvis and his agents surrounded Dillinger. Every person who was there seemed to tell a different story of how it happened, but John Dillinger was shot dead and two bystanders suffered minor injuries.

Soon Pretty Boy and Baby Face would meet the same fate. In fact, it was Purvis who led the party that tracked Floyd to a farm near East Liverpool, Ohio, on October 22. As Floyd tried to flee, Purvis gave the command to fire, and Floyd fell to the ground wounded. He died as Purvis tried to question him. Agents from the Chicago office commanded by Purvis also tracked down Baby Face on November 27. Racing down an Illinois highway, two agents exchanged gunfire with Baby Face and his accomplice, John Paul Chase. Although the two gangsters eluded the agents, another car carrying two more FBI agents caught up with them. The agents followed the car into a park, where Baby Face and Chase ambushed them. Although both FBI agents were killed, they also managed to take down Baby Face Nelson.

With some of the nation's most famous gangsters in their graves, the authorities continued to track down their accomplices and other gangsters. As the FBI and police forces were getting better at catching criminals, the prison population began to increase, and the government began to look at ways to keep the most notorious criminals and escape artists behind bars.

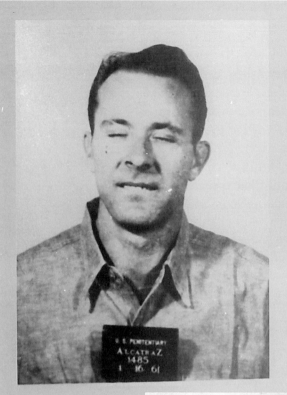

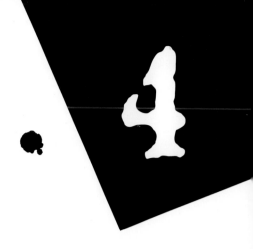

Escape from "The Rock"

The Daring Alcatraz Escape of 1962

In the waning days of the gangster era, more and more criminals were being sent to prison, but unfortunately, more and more criminals were escaping from prison. With even maximum-security prisons in Atlanta, Georgia, and Leavenworth, Kansas, suffering from violence and escape attempts, the federal Bureau of Prisons wanted to make a statement. There was one place that seemed perfect not only to create a new prison with stricter security measures than anything that came before it, but also to offer a vivid warning to criminals and potential criminals. That place was Alcatraz.

Located in the cold, choppy waters of the San Francisco Bay, Alcatraz earned the nickname "Devil's Island." Surrounded by rock walls, the island looked like it was designed by nature to be a fortress; in fact, it was used for many years for just that purpose. The rough waters and rocky coastline also made the island perfect as a prison. The federal government built a cell house there

One of the most daring prison breaks in history was carried out by Clarence Anglin (left), John Anglin (center), and Frank Lee Morris (right) in 1962. Using a series of tunnels and a homemade raft, the three escaped from Alcatraz and set out across San Francisco Bay. None were ever heard from again.

Built on an island in San Francisco Bay, Alcatraz (also known as "the Rock") was considered escape-proof. The Anglin brothers and Frank Lee Morris proved otherwise, and although their bodies wee never recovered, many believe they drowned in the bay's strong currents.

in 1909, using it to house military prisoners. However, when the Bureau of Prisons took over, it made major changes that transformed "the Rock" into the toughest prison in the nation. New features included tear gas canisters suspended from the ceiling of the dining hall; cell bars that were wider and flatter, making them more difficult to saw; electric eyes and listening systems; and automatic locks. The only door out of the cell house was reinforced and heavily guarded, and tall towers, catwalks, and plenty of barbed wire secured the grounds.

The operations of the prison were also designed to minimize any chance of escape. When the Bureau of Prisons took over in 1934, it conducted a nationwide search for the best personnel and subjected them to rigorous training and physical conditioning. No unauthorized boats were allowed anywhere near the island. When the prison first opened, the prisoners were subject to strict policies that hearkened back to an earlier era: visits were strictly limited, mail was censored, and the prisoners were not allowed to speak in the dining hall.

Slowly, the Bureau of Prisons began to transfer the worst criminals in the system to Alcatraz. The prison's first warden, James A. Johnston, recalls:

> It seemed as if most of the established escape artists had been corralled in the federal net and transferred to Alcatraz in our first five years from 1934 to 1938, but more kept coming with every group every year . . .
>
> One time the record clerk made a graph for me that showed seventy per cent of our population had escaped from some form of custody. In the circumstances I instructed our officers to count their shop and cell house details frequently and to regard every inmate as a possible escapee.

The Rock's most notorious prisoner was Alphonse "Scarface" Capone, who ruled an empire of organized crime in Chicago. Under his direction, his gang controlled bootlegging, gambling, and other illegal activities in what was then the nation's second largest city. Although his gang was blamed for the "St. Valentine's Day Massacre," in which seven members of a rival gang were gunned down, Capone eventually went to prison after being convicted of not paying enough income tax. Some of the other "celebrity" prisoners at Alcatraz included kidnappers George "Machine Gun" Kelly, Arthur "Dock" Barker, and Alvin "Old Creepy" Karpis. However, none of these high-profile criminals received any special treatment, and Capone even had the humiliating job of mopping the prison floors.

Barker fared worse: he was shot to death by guards

while trying to escape in 1939, one of a dozen escape attempts that had occurred by the start of the 1960s. The most notable attempt had been the "battle of Alcatraz" in 1946, during which guards shot and killed five prisoners. But no one had escaped during the battle; in fact, no one had ever escaped when four men joined together to pull off one of the most innovative and intricate escape attempts in history on June 11, 1962.

Allen West, Frank Lee Morris, and brothers John and Clarence Anglin had a lot in common. All of them had served time in Raiford State Prison in Florida and the federal penitentiary in Atlanta. As criminals, none of them was very good: Morris once was caught with jars and jars of change after stealing $6,500 in coins from a bank, and the others each had his own story of carelessness. Prison violence, escape attempts, or both had landed each of them in Alcatraz. After being reunited on the Rock, they put their heads together for months planning what they hoped would be the first successful escape from Alcatraz.

With all of its strengths, Alcatraz also had its weaknesses. West did most of the work in discovering those weaknesses and how to exploit them. Because there was no way to escape through the heavily guarded front door, West had to find another way out. Quietly, to avoid suspicion, West began asking around among the older inmates if they knew of any options. Some of the men who had been at Alcatraz the longest remembered that there used to be air vents in the ceiling, but they had been filled in with concrete. West investigated this lead. According to one of the convicts who had done electrical work, one of the vents had not been filled in with concrete, but had bars instead.

West had discovered a way out, but it was definitely not an easy way out. The vent was located above Cellblock B. One of the prison's four main blocks of cells, Cellblock B contained three stories of cells that had concrete on three sides. On the front of the cells were iron bars and narrow walkways. It was along these walkways that the guard walked at regular intervals, checking on the prisoners. On top of the cellblock was enough room for someone to walk around under the ceiling. A utility corridor ran behind the cells, supplying each with water and electricity, and removing wastewater. Because Alcatraz was an island in the middle of saltwater, fresh water was expensive, and therefore saltwater was used in the toilets.

This utility corridor, with its saltwater pipes, proved to be another weakness that West would exploit in his plan. From another convict who had worked as a plumber's assistant, West learned that the concrete walls in the utility corridor were in bad shape, caused by years of exposure to saltwater. The saltwater had caused the pipes to deteriorate, leaking and sometimes bursting. The saltwater then seeped into the concrete, eroding the surface and making it easier to break.

West was getting great information from other convicts, but he needed a way to look around. The best bet seemed to be to work in prison maintenance, which took a prisoner all over the prison doing tedious and unpleasant jobs. Other prisoners hated it, but it was the perfect job for a person who was trying to escape. With his new job, West was in a great position to get access to all areas of the prison, and even got to see the inside of the utility corridor, but he needed some help.

A number of convicts were originally involved in the plot to escape—probably more people than were ever discovered. Although many convicts aided the plotters, several became nervous and decided that they no longer wanted to try to break out. Only three other prisoners, Morris and the Anglin brothers, stuck with the plan to escape. One by one, they made sure that they were assigned to Cellblock B, and by September 1961, all four men were on the cellblock with the vulnerable air vent.

Like West, each of the other three men had a prison job that would help in the escape. Morris' job in "industries"—the shop in which the convicts manufactured brooms and other items for sales—provided obvious benefits. Although the convicts passed through a metal detector at the end of each day, the metal detectors of the time were not very sensitive, and he was able to smuggle small pieces of metal from the shop. Surprisingly, Clarence's work as a barber and John's job in the clothing room would also prove to be useful as the plan progressed.

In the early 1960s, society was beginning to change. Just as the civil rights movement was gaining momentum on the "outside," people were also pushing for prison reform. Alcatraz had earned a reputation for being in terrible condition, and under Warden Olin Blackwell, repairs and improvements were being made. Because many of the jobs required a great deal of expertise, outside tradesmen came to the prison. However, they often used inmates as helpers, and some less difficult jobs were given directly to inmates. One project—painting the prison's ceiling—could not have been a more perfect opportunity for West.

For quite some time, West worked atop a scaffold, which provided him with a means of climbing to the ceiling and standing on a platform as he worked. He could see the air vent, and he knew that there was room to walk around on top of the cellblocks. Somehow, he managed to persuade one of the guards to let him on top of the cellblocks and work there unwatched. However, he saved the most important spot—the area above Cellblock B—for last.

West knew that the utility corridor was the perfect escape route because it was filled with pipes that could be climbed to the top of the cellblock. However, the men needed to find a way into the utility corridor from their cells. Each cell had a small metal vent that was only 5 inches tall and 9 ½ inches wide—certainly not an opening big enough for a man to crawl through. But knowing that the concrete walls behind them were slowly crumbling, the men decided that they could dig their way out.

Each man began to dig an opening around the vent

in his cell. How the men drilled these holes is a matter that is still debated today. The "official" explanation, which prison officials gave at the time, and which tour guides continue to give now that Alcatraz has been converted into a national park, is that the men used sharpened spoon handles. They worked at the only time when guards would not hear them—the "happy hour" after supper, during which the convicts were allowed to play musical instruments. The sound of dozens of convicts playing dozens of different tunes at once, with varying levels of skill, was enough to cover up their actions.

Others doubt that the men could have possibly made it out using spoons. One guard who previously had been stationed at Alcatraz speculated that they must have smuggled a masonry drill bit, which is designed for concrete and brick, into their cells and turned the bit by hand. The gangster Alvin Karpis, who played a minor role in the escape attempt, had another explanation, claiming that that convicts had used the cover of the repairs to make the holes:

> The truth is that the authorities were too embarrassed to admit that the holes were cut from the utility corridors behind the cells where the inmates had been left alone with jackhammers while the careless guards avoided the discomfort of the dust in the air.

Regardless of how the prisoners made the holes in the wall, they carefully covered their work to avoid detection by the guards. They had to improvise with whatever supplies they could get their hands on. They first plugged the small drill holes with soap and toilet paper and then covered their work with matching green paint that West had stolen while working his maintenance job. They later made replicas of the grates and the surrounding wall space, using cardboard, wood, tobacco boxes, and canvas art board. They did a remarkably convincing job, and the guards never noticed that anything was wrong.

As they came closer to being able to break free of their cells, they started thinking ahead: how would they get off the island? With its strong current and chilly water, the San Francisco Bay would not be easy to swim; they decided that they would need a raft and life vests. Suddenly, John's position in the clothing room was a key element to the plot. The men devised a complicated system for stealing raincoats, stripping out the rubber lining, and then smuggling the rubber lining into industries, where conspirators sewed straps onto the vests.

The life vests' seams were sealed with rubber cement, but the vests would probably lose air. Another convict had the answer to this problem. At the neckline of each vest was a plastic tube from a spray bottle of window cleaner. The person wearing the vest could lean down and blow air into the vest. A heavy paper clip was used to seal off the tube. Plans for the life vests were already underway when, by a remarkable coincidence, the March 1962 issues of *Popular Science* and *Popular Mechanics* arrived at the prison, each containing articles about life vests.

On April 25, John Anglin finally made it out of his cell and into the utility corridor, and by May 11 his brother Clarence and Frank Lee Morris had also broken free. But they had several challenges ahead of them. They still had to break through the bars on the air vent and make their life raft; therefore, they needed access to the top of the cellblock. How could they do this and avoid detection? If a guard noticed them missing from their cells, or saw them on top of the cellblock, then they would be caught and their hopes of escape would be dashed.

Their strategy for preventing the guards from noticing their absence became legendary. They began obtaining materials, such as electrical wire, cement, plaster, and oil paint from other inmates. Working with clippings of hair that Clarence had secretly collected from the barbershop, they began working—perhaps aided by more artistic inmates—on what would be the centerpiece of their escape attempt. They actually

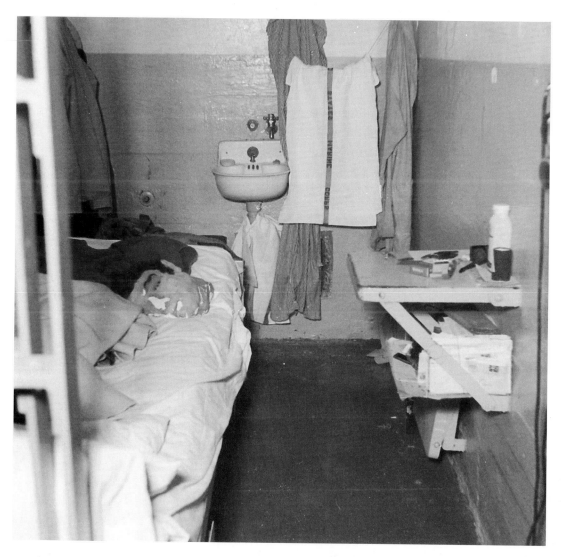

made replicas of their own heads! Each time they needed to leave their cells during "happy hour," they put rolled-up blankets in their beds and the fake heads on their pillows. Although upon close inspection, the heads are not very lifelike, they fooled the guards walking by their cells.

Through West's ingenuity and cunning, he actually managed to get the men a private workshop on top of the cellblock. While working on the ceiling painting

To facilitate their escape, the Anglin brothers and Frank Lee Morris created dummy heads for themselves, which they then placed in their prison cots to fool the guards who made regular bed checks.

project, he had tried his best to develop a rapport with the guard who was supervising him, Jerry Herring. Having waited until they were ready to work on the grate, he finally informed Herring that he needed to paint the ceiling above Cellblock B. West then created a diversion by sweeping dirt off the side of the cellblock. When the prison lieutenant discovered the dirt all over the floors, he questioned Herring. Somehow, West convinced Herring that the answer to the problem was to hang blankets around the area in which he was working.

The men now could slip out of their cells undetected and work on top of the cellblock without being seen. However, they still had plenty of work to do, had to do it with improvised tools, and had to be quiet enough not to be heard over the wailing music during happy hour. They devised a system for bringing supplies up to their workshop. One man would climb the pipes and drop a string down to the other men. They used this system to bring up all their supplies, including the life vests, raincoat material for the raft, handmade wooden paddles, and even a vacuum cleaner motor that another convict had stolen for them.

Morris' job was to get through the two sets of bars securing the ceiling vent. Although Morris had hoped that he could use the vacuum cleaner motor and stolen bits to make a drill, the motor was not strong enough. He had to get through the bars under his own power. The first set of bars bent easily: Morris used a "bar spreader," which had long been used in prison escapes. The bar spreader is a handmade tool operated by placing it between two bars and then turning a nut to make it expand; slowly, the prison bars spread apart. The second set of bars was more challenging. He had to saw through the steel rivets that held the bars to the vent.

In the meantime, the Anglin brothers worked on the raft. They had originally planned to make a square raft, but without discussing it with Morris and West, the two brothers decided instead to make a triangular raft. They defended their design, saying that they knew about rafting on rivers. The other men were upset and thought that the design would not work for four people. However, there was no time to build a new raft: Herring had been asking West questions about the blankets. They were stuck with their triangular raft, which they would inflate with an accordion that Morris had purchased while in prison.

When Morris finally broke through the bars on the vent, the four men were ready to go. On the night of June 11, each man pushed out his fake wall, left a mask in his place, and went into the utility corridor—each man except West, that is. Of the four men, only West had never actually tested his escape hatch. When the time came, the man who masterminded the whole plan could not make it out of his cell. By the time Morris learned of his predicament, the Anglin brothers were already on top of the cellblock. West pleaded with Morris to get the other men to help dig. Morris climbed up the pipes to the top of the cellblock, but West never saw him again.

Between 10:00 and 10:30 P.M., a guard heard a loud crashing sound coming from the top of the prison. He reported it to the control room, where the staff used the electronic listening devices to monitor different parts of the prison. However, they did not hear any more suspicious noises, and nobody was sent to investigate. They could not imagine that it was the sound of the cover of the air vent crashing onto the roof. Ironically, the one watchtower that had a good view of that portion of the roof had just closed the previous month as a cost-saving measure. When West finally managed to make it to the roof at about 1:45 A.M., the men were long gone, and without a raft, he could not follow them.

The masks did their job. It was not until after the 7:00 A.M. wake-up bell the next morning that the

Here a guard examines a hole used by the Alcatraz escapees to gain access to a duct. One of the most elaborate escapes in U.S. prison history, it still remains shrouded in mystery.

guards knew that anything was wrong. Karpis recalls the discovery of the fake heads by "Sarge" Bartlett:

Today three prisoners are still curled up in their bunks. Swearing to himself, Sarge reaches into each of the cells shaking the pillows under the sleeping bodies. It's at the third cell that he grabs the con by the hair, prepared to jerk him awake. The head rolls from the bunk onto the hard concrete floor. Sarge screams for help, believing in the confused seconds of discovery that someone has grotesquely severed the head from its body.

Nobody at Alcatraz ever saw Frank Lee Morris, Clarence Anglin, or John Anglin again. To this day, people debate whether or not they made it out alive. Although searchers found papers, life vests, and a paddle, they never found the raft, or any of the three men's bodies. Whether they made it through the cold, choppy waters of the San Francisco Bay might never be known, but the three men had made it off the island in one of the most ingenious escapes in prison history. No longer considered inescapable, the federal penitentiary at Alcatraz closed on March 21, 1963.

A Voice
for Freedom
Is Silenced

The Assassination of
Rev. Martin Luther King, Jr.

During the 1960s, the United States went through a number of dramatic changes. It was a time of protest, as many people began to question authority. People protested against war, nuclear weapons, and especially against racism. Although the U.S. Supreme Court had made it clear that all citizens deserve equal rights under the law, many white people, including politicians and police officers, continued to discriminate against African-Americans. The civil rights movement was an effort among African-Americans to gain equal access to opportunities such as education, jobs, and government positions.

The most prominent leader of the movement was Rev. Martin Luther King, Jr., who supported non-violent ways of protesting against the establishment. In his most famous speech, King expressed his hopes that African-Americans could convince the country to live

The cause of civil rights in America lost one of its most charismatic and successful leaders with the assassination of Dr. Martin Luther King, Jr. in Memphis in 1968. This memorial to the slain civil rights leader remains in Atlanta, GA.

Dr. King's advocacy of nonviolent protest earned him worldwide notice and respect. At this 1963 march in Washington D.C., protestors rally to end school segregation, obtain fair voting rights, and to improve employment opportunities for African-Americans.

up to the ideals expressed in the Declaration of Independence nearly two centuries earlier. "I have a dream that one day this nation will rise up and live out the true meaning of its creed; 'We hold these truths to be self-evident, that all men are created equal,'" he told a crowd in Washington, D.C., in 1963.

Some people did not share King's dream. The decade was a time of political change, but it was also a time when desperate people tried to resist that change. Sometimes these people resorted to violence against the people who most actively and powerfully supported change. During the 1960s, assassins killed President John F. Kennedy; his brother, Robert Kennedy; and civil rights leaders Medgar Evers, Malcolm X, and—on April 4, 1968—Rev. Martin Luther King, Jr.

In early 1968, King was devoting much of his effort to leading the Poor People's Campaign. In an effort to bring thousands of unemployed African-Americans to Washington, D.C., to protest economic and social injustices, King traveled to recruit demonstrators and train them in the art of non-violent protest. However, fate would soon intervene, bringing him to Memphis, Tennessee. The sanitation workers who were responsible for collecting and hauling the city's garbage were unhappy with their working conditions. African-American workers were especially unhappy. One day during a rainstorm, supervisors had sent each of the workers home; white employees had received a full day's pay, but the African-American workers had been paid for only two hours. This was exactly the type of racism that King and his colleagues were trying to eliminate from government and society. When the sanitation workers called a strike—a stoppage of work—to protest their working conditions, King felt that he should go to Memphis to support the strikes.

Turning his attention from the Poor People's Campaign, King made several trips to Memphis. On his first trip, he addressed a large crowd of people; many African-Americans in Memphis supported the strike. He told his enthusiastic audience that he would return to lead a protest against the city. Although delayed slightly by an unexpected snowstorm, King returned on March 28. A crowd of several thousand people had showed up to follow King and the sanitation workers on a march down the streets of Memphis to City Hall.

King had planned a non-violent protest, but other people had not. A group called the Invaders, as well as some other young people, had decided to use the march as a cover for wreaking havoc. As the march passed historic Beale Street, chaos suddenly erupted. A group of youths led by the Invaders began smashing store windows and looting the merchants. The mayor called the National Guard, and 3,500 troops marched in an attempt to restore order. Over 300 people were arrested, and four people were shot, one of whom died. King and his colleagues had fled, horrified that the peaceful protest they had planned had turned violent.

For the next few days, Memphis was in disarray. With the city operating under a curfew requiring everyone to be inside by 7:00 P.M., conditions for African-Americans had not improved. King knew that he had to lead another march in Memphis, and that this time it would have to be peaceful. Fearing more violence, the city tried to stop the march, getting a judge to issue a "restraining order" that legally prevented King from leading another protest. The Memphis police set up a stakeout at a fire station near the Lorraine Motel, where King was staying. On April 3, King's aides went to court to try to have the restraining order overturned, but King was determined to lead the march no matter what happened.

King never had the chance to lead another march. On the evening of April 4, King and his close friend, Rev. Ralph David Abernathy, were getting ready to go to a local minister's house for supper. King went out onto the balcony and began chatting about the weather with the driver waiting to take the men to supper; the driver advised King to wear an overcoat. Suddenly, the driver heard a loud shot and saw King slump to the floor. Abernathy had also heard the shot and found King lying on the balcony, bleeding from his neck and barely alive. Although an ambulance rushed King to the hospital, doctors were not able to save his life.

Throughout the nation, people reacted in anger to King's slaying. In many cities, there were riots, as people smashed windows, set fires, and committed acts of violence against other people. Dozens of people

died, and more than 20,000 people were arrested. While several major cities mobilized Army and National Guard troops, King's close friends pleaded for the rioters to stop. President Lyndon B. Johnson declared April 7 to be a national day of mourning. Slowly, the rioting stopped, but King's life and death had changed America forever. Congress passed new civil rights laws, and today King is remembered with a national holiday.

At the crime scene, local police and the FBI began their search for the killer. Many people indicated that the shot had come from Bessie Brewer's rooming house. This low-rent boarding home had its rear windows across the street from the Lorraine, but its front door was actually on another street, which meant that the assassin could have fired a bullet from one of the windows and then

On the Memphis balcony where he would soon face an assassin's bullet, Dr. King (right center) stands with other civil rights leaders, including Hosea Williams (left), Jesse Jackson (left center), and Ralph Abernathy (right).

escaped unnoticed while everyone congregated around the Lorraine's parking lot.

According to Brewer, a mysterious new tenant had arrived that day. She first showed him a room with a stove and refrigerator near the front of the boarding home, but he then told her that he wanted just a bedroom. He was pleased when she showed him a room at the rear of the building. When she showed the room to investigators, they noticed that furniture had been moved away from a window, which would allow the occupant to view the Lorraine motel. Brewer and other tenants described the new tenant as a neatly dressed white man, just under six feet tall, with a slim to medium build.

Based on what they learned from the other tenants, investigators believed that the new tenant had fired the fatal shot from the window of the hallway bathroom. The bathroom had a much better view of the Lorraine, and one of the tenants mentioned that he noticed that the bathroom had been occupied for long periods of time that day, but that he had not heard water running. Immediately after the shot, he and another tenant saw a man— believed to be the new tenant—running from the bathroom carrying a bundle.

The bundle was found near the front door of the rooming house. Witnesses heard a thud against the window of a nearby business and then saw a white Ford Mustang speed away. Wrapped in a blanket was a high-powered rifle with a telescopic sight, a pair of binoculars, and some clothing. Investigators had not only the murder weapon, but evidence that they hoped would help them to track down the killer. Detectives traced the binoculars to a store in Memphis and the rifle to a store in Birmingham, Alabama. Both salespeople gave a description similar to the one given by the tenants at the rooming house.

Acting on the information they had gathered, the police and FBI were searching for a white male, possibly driving a white Mustang, and possibly with ties to Birmingham. They made their first break in tracking down their suspect when they learned that someone named Eric Starvo Galt had stayed in the Rebel Motel in Memphis the night before the murder. He had given a Birmingham address, and he drove a Mustang with Alabama plates. The state of Alabama confirmed that Galt had registered a Mustang, and according to his driver's license, he was 5'11", weighed 175 pounds, and had brown hair and blue eyes. His address was another low-rent rooming house; people there did not know much about Galt. The residents said that he mostly kept to himself, but that he had taken dance lessons. This would prove to be a crucial piece of information.

In addition to their Alabama investigation, FBI agents were also searching for clues in Los Angeles, California. The clothing found at the crime scene bore markings from a laundry service in Los Angeles; the laundry's records indicated that Galt had lived at another cheap rooming house. Acting on the unusual information that Galt had taken dance lessons in Birmingham, the detectives soon learned that Galt had taken lessons in Los Angeles as well. The dance instructor remembered Galt, saying that he was also taking bartending lessons. The FBI then made a major break in solving the case: a local bartending school not only had records of Eric Starvo Galt, it also had his graduation picture.

Meanwhile, the FBI was conducting investigations in yet another city: Galt's Mustang had been found in Atlanta, Georgia. Thinking that Galt might be staying in a cheap rooming house like the ones in Birmingham and Los Angeles, detectives began their search. They did not find Galt, but they did find a rooming house where he had stayed in late March. Galt had left behind an important piece of evidence: a map of Atlanta with circles over the locations of King's home and his organization, the Southern Christian Leadership Conference (SCLC). The FBI was able to retrieve a fingerprint from the map, which matched those on the rifle and the binoculars found at the crime scene.

Although by 1968, the FBI had made many improvements in its ability to fight crime, the process of tracking someone by his or her fingerprints was still a slow process. Before the development of computerized fingerprint matching, it had to be done by hand. To help narrow down the process a bit, the FBI took a guess that Galt might have escaped from prison—he certainly moved around a lot. It was a lucky guess: the FBI identified the fingerprints as those of James Earl Ray, who had escaped from Missouri State Penitentiary in April 1967.

The FBI now knew that Eric Starvo Galt was really James Earl Ray, and they began a national search for the prime suspect in the killing of the civil rights leader. While interviewing Ray's acquaintances, agents learned that Ray had expressed hatred toward African-Americans, and some even claimed that he had talked about killing King. Not surprisingly, the FBI had little luck obtaining information from Ray's family, but a former cellmate at Missouri State Penitentiary provided an important lead. While in prison, Ray had often talked about how easy it was to obtain a fake passport in Canada.

At the FBI's request, the Royal Canadian Mounted Police conducted a painstaking search of recent passport applications, trying to find one that might be Ray's. An application for a passport recently issued to Ramon George Sneyd aroused their attention, and based on a photograph submitted with the application, as well as fingerprints on the application, that Ramon George Sneyd was also really James Earl Ray. Although Ray was using a new alias, the manhunt, which was now international, was closing in on him. Tracing Ray's fake passport, the FBI tracked him from Toronto, Canada, to London, England, and then to Lisbon, Portugal, and back to London. In London, officers of New Scotland Yard were on alert, looking for someone traveling under the name of Ramon George Sneyd.

On June 8, an official at London's airport stopped a Belgium-bound passenger who seemed to have two

After an extensive investigation, James Earl Ray was arrested, tried, and convicted for the murder of Dr. Martin Luther King, Jr. Despite appeals for parole, Ray remained in prison for 30 years, until his death in 1998.

passports. Looking at a list of people to watch for, the official noticed that Ramon George Sneyd was on that list. When police officers interrogated him, they discovered that he had been trying to carry a handgun onto the flight; meanwhile, they confirmed that their detainee, James Earl Ray, was on the FBI's wanted list. Facing a mountain of evidence, Ray and his lawyers tried to prevent his extradition, or transfer to a U.S. jail. However, they lost the legal battle, and a group of FBI agents brought Ray to a Memphis jail; they flew late at night on an Air Force plane as a precaution against anyone who might try to kill Ray.

While awaiting trial, Ray began to claim that he acted as part of a conspiracy—that other people were involved in the plot to kill King. Many Americans believed that there had been a conspiracy. As someone who wanted to change society, King had made many enemies among racist groups. Groups such as the Ku Klux Klan had openly expressed their hatred of the civil rights leader. King also had his enemies within the government, even within the FBI, which had hunted down James Earl Ray. Perceiving King as a threat to "law and order," Director J. Edgar Hoover had publicly criticized King, and the FBI had spied on King's activities.

People eagerly anticipated Ray's murder trial, hoping that they would learn more about the conspiracy. But in a shocking move, Ray pled guilty in March 1969, four weeks before his trial was set to begin. Ray's confession did little to stop speculation of a conspiracy, and even after confessing, Ray continued to fuel the speculation. He implicated a mysterious character named "Raoul." However, Ray's stories were not consistent: sometimes, he said that he drove the getaway car after Raoul fired the fatal shot, and other times, he said that he was at a gas station while the murder occurred. In another version, Ray acted on behalf of the FBI, who left him to "take the fall" for the crime.

Because of Ray's accusations against the FBI, the Department of Justice (DOJ) later appointed an independent task force to investigate whether Ray had acted as part of a conspiracy. The task force found Ray's "varying and patently self-serving tales to be unbelievable" and "concluded that Ray was lying about the existence of a 'Raoul.'" However, the report left a major question unanswered. During the time that passed between Ray's 1967 escape from prison and the time he was arrested for King's murder, he traveled widely, bought an expensive car and camera equipment, and took various classes: where did he get the money? His family was not wealthy, nor could he be linked to any crimes that could have supported his lifestyle. The DOJ reported admitted that "the sources for Ray's funds still remain a mystery . . ." but nonetheless found no evidence of a conspiracy.

Despite the official reports, many people continue to believe that Ray did not act alone. In addition to the Department of Justice investigation, the Senate held hearings about the assassination, and numerous books, television shows, and "mock trials" tried to expose the "truth" of what happened. Ray fought for years to get a trial; even the King family supported Ray's efforts, hoping that the trial would expose information that Ray had kept secret for many years. However, when Ray died in April 1998, any secrets that he might have had died with him.

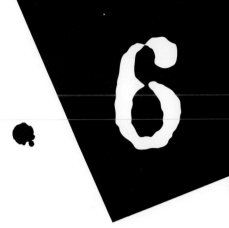

A BREAK-IN BRINGS DOWN A PRESIDENT

*The Watergate Burglary and
President Richard Nixon's Resignation*

*In a crime that shook the
faith of Americans in their
leaders, the Watergate
scandal of the mid-1970s
eventually led to the
resignation of President
Richard M. Nixon and
the conviction and impris-
onment of many of his
top aides.*

As the 1960s ended, America hoped for an end to the political turmoil that had marked the past decade, but early in the new decade a scandal changed the presidency forever. In 1974, Richard M. Nixon became the first president to resign his office. Nixon's downfall came as a result of the "Watergate" scandal, so-named for a burglary attempt at the Watergate building complex in Washington, D.C. Although the burglary was unsuccessful and the burglars were caught at the scene, it became one of the most significant crimes of the century because of its impact on the presidency and the public. The burglary was funded by Nixon's presidential campaign, and its purpose was to spy on the rival Democratic Party's campaign. In the months following the burglary, President Nixon and his top aides would try everything to conceal his campaign's involvement with the burglary. The efforts included misleading the FBI, the courts, the U.S. Congress, and the American public.

Throughout the years, Nixon's political career had its ups and downs. In the 1940s and 1950s, he rose quickly through the political ranks. In 1946 and 1948, he was elected to the U.S. House of Representatives. As his second term in the lower house of Congress expired, he won election to the U.S. Senate in 1950. Before his six-year term ended, however, Dwight D. Eisenhower selected him as his vice-presidential running mate, and Nixon was elected to two terms as U.S. vice president in 1952 and 1956. However, in the early 1960s, Nixon's career fell as rapidly as it had risen in the previous two decades. In 1960, he lost the presidential election to Democrat John F. Kennedy. Then in 1962, he lost the election for governor of California. Telling reporters that they would not have Nixon to kick around any more, he went into private law practice.

However, Nixon longed for a return to national politics. He waited until the 1968 election before seeking and winning the Republican Party's nomination as its candidate in the presidential election. That November, he defeated Democrat Hubert H. Humphrey in a close race. Stung by electoral losses in 1960 and 1962, and a narrow victory in 1968, Nixon was greatly concerned with re-election during his presidency—some would say that he was obsessed with "campaign intelligence," or learning what the other candidates were doing. It was Nixon's hunger for campaign intelligence that ultimately led to his August 9, 1974, resignation from office.

On June 17, 1972, Democrat George McGovern was the leading candidate for his party's nomination to run against Nixon in the November election. During the early morning hours, a group of five men broke into the Watergate headquarters of the Democratic National Committee, which was devoted to helping a Democrat defeat Nixon in the upcoming election. The intruders brought with them a variety of spy equipment, including

cameras and electronic bugging devices, which can secretly record conversations. They also carried large amounts of cash.

Dressed neatly in business suits, the burglars also wore surgical gloves, being careful not to leave behind any fingerprints. However, an act of carelessness led to their detection by a security guard and arrest by local police. To enter the building, the burglars put pieces of tape over several door locks so that they could easily open the doors without keys. A night watchman discovered one of these pieces of tape but simply removed it. He did not call the police until he returned later and saw that the door had been re-taped, making him suspect that burglars had taped the door.

Police responded to the security guard's call almost

The Watergate scandal began with a small, seemingly unimportant event. A security guard at Washington's Watergate Hotel noticed a small piece of tape on a door lock to the Democratic National Committee's head-quarters. Further investigation of the burglary uncovered a plot that led to the highest levels of government.

immediately and arrested the five men. When the burglars appeared before a judge, it was revealed that one of the five, James McCord, was an employee of the Committee to Re-elect the President (CRP or "CREEP"), which was in charge of Nixon's campaign for the November 1972 presidential election. Two other men were later charged with participating in the burglary. G. Gordon Liddy and E. Howard Hunt, Jr., helped plan the crime, and they had been in contact, by walkie-talkie, during the break-in. Like McCord, both Liddy and Hunt had ties to President Nixon. Liddy was CRP's campaign finance lawyer, and Hunt had served as a consultant to the White House.

Many of President Nixon's closest advisors were heavily involved in covering up the White House's involvement in the Watergate break-in. Presidential aides arranged payments to the burglars in the hopes of buying their silence. Leonard Garment, who was a lawyer in the Nixon White House, explains: "Within hours of the arrest of the Watergate burglars, everyone connected with the campaign intelligence activities of which they were a part knew that there had been a disaster and began—unthinkingly, in the manner of most human beings—to try to cover up their mess."

The FBI traced some of the money carried by the burglars to a Miami bank account into which the CRP had deposited funds raised for the Nixon campaign. When the FBI began to trace the source of the money used to finance the Watergate burglary, the President himself—as it would later be revealed—became involved in the cover-up.

At Nixon's request, his aide H.R. Haldeman met with Vernon Walters, deputy director of the Central Intelligence Agency (CIA). The CIA is in charge of protecting the United State's interests in other countries, through spying and other activities. Haldeman instructed Walters to request that FBI director Patrick Gray call off the Watergate investigation, using the excuse that the investigation threatened the CIA's security interests in Mexico. Although Walters knew that the investigation did not compromise CIA security, he nonetheless made the request to Gray, who in turn called off the investigation.

With the FBI investigation stalled, the President continued to deny any White House involvement in the Watergate burglary. However, Walters and Gray soon discussed their misgivings about the White House's request, and on July 6, 1972, Gray told the President that the FBI had decided to continue its investigation. To help insure that the FBI's investigation did not implicate the White House, Nixon's top aides worked to buy the silence of the Watergate burglars. The aides arranged for payments to the burglars and even hinted that the President would exercise his power to pardon the men for their crimes if they pled guilty without implicating the White House.

Despite the efforts of reporters at major newspapers to dig more deeply into the Watergate controversy, the cover-up remained successful through the November 1972 presidential election. The cover-up was so successful, in fact, that Nixon won the general election by a landslide—beating Democratic candidate George McGovern by over 18 million popular votes.

Even through the trial for the Watergate burglary—in which five of the men pled guilty and McCord and Liddy were convicted—the cover-up remained successful. Judge John Sirica sensed, however, that there was a conspiracy much broader than the seven men before his court. When the trial ended on January 30, 1973, Judge Sirica announced that he would postpone giving the men their prison sentences until March. He hoped that some of the seven men would offer information about the conspiracy in exchange for lighter sentences. Before the March 23, 1973, sentencing, McCord finally broke his silence, as did others involved with the burglary, with the exception of Liddy. The burglars tied the conspiracy to

Nixon's top advisors, many of whom resigned by the end of April 1973.

With Nixon's advisors resigning in droves, it became clear to everyone that the Nixon campaign had funded the burglary at the Watergate in hopes of learning Democratic campaign secrets. It was also clear that the White House staff had tried to cover up its involvement with the crime. And although many people suspected that President Nixon had been involved personally, he remained solid in his denials.

As Senator Ervin finally began his hearings, the Department of Justice, which handles federal criminal prosecutions, also became involved. The department had a new head: Elliot Richardson had recently replaced the former Attorney General, who had resigned because of his role in the scandal. One of Richardson's first official acts was to appoint Harvard Law School professor Archibald Cox as special prosecutor. Cox was to have the ability to investigate Watergate matters independently of the Attorney General, who is a presidential appointee and therefore might be biased in favor of the president. Although both Cox and Senator Ervin were pursuing Nixon, the President continued to deny involvement in the Watergate burglary and cover-up. However, the heat on the President increased with two important developments in June and July of 1973.

In June, John Dean, who had resigned as the White House's top lawyer, testified before the Ervin committee that the President had personal knowledge of the Watergate burglary soon after it happened and had personally participated in the cover-up. However, Dean was the only witness to implicate the President directly, and Nixon denied the truth of Dean's testimony.

In July, the Ervin committee made a startling discovery—President Nixon had taped many of his conversations in the Oval Office. Immediately, a battle began for the tapes, with both Ervin and Cox seeking to have the tapes turned over. Nixon argued that, as President, the Constitution protected him from being required to turn over the tapes. In Nixon's own words:

> Unless a President can protect the privacy of the advice he gets, he cannot get the advice he needs.
>
> This principle is recognized in the constitutional doctrine of executive privilege, which has been defended and maintained by every President since Washington and which has been recognized by the courts whenever tested . . .

On Saturday evening, October 20, 1973, with Cox continuing to demand the White House tapes, Nixon made a desperate move that doomed his presidency. He ordered Attorney General Richardson to fire Cox as special prosecutor. Because Cox was supposed to be conducting an independent investigation, Richardson refused to fire him and resigned instead. Richardson's Deputy Attorney General also refused to fire Cox and also resigned. Finally, Solicitor General Robert Bork, third in command at the Justice Department, fired Cox.

In firing the Watergate special prosecutor, Nixon grossly overestimated his support by the American public:

> What came to be known as the "Saturday Night Massacre" [because so many important people lost their jobs] then unleashed the torrent of public anger at Nixon that had been building across the nation. In a period of ten days, more than a million letters and telegrams descended on members of Congress, almost all of them demanding Nixon's impeachment. Before long, according to some, there were three million letters and telegrams, and an impeachment inquiry was begun.

On November 17, Nixon told the nation, "I am not a crook." But as time wore on, more and more people began to believe that Nixon was a crook. Reluctantly, Nixon's lawyers began to turn over tapes to Judge Sirica. As many expected, the tapes raised the suspicion that the President was involved in covering up the Watergate burglary. On November 21, 1973, Nixon's attorneys informed Judge Sirica of an 18½-minute gap on the tape made on Nixon's first day back in the White House after the Watergate burglary. (He had been vacationing on the island of Bermuda when the burglary took place.)

Once the 18½-minute gap was revealed, there was widespread speculation that the president and aide H.R. Haldeman had discussed the burglary and planned a cover-up on June 20, 1972, just days after the crime took place. Nixon's lawyers could not offer Judge Sirica an adequate explanation, recalls attorney Leonard Garment:

> On January 15, 1974, a panel of experts appointed by Judge Sirica concluded that that 18½-minute gap was the product of what appeared to be five separate, deliberate erasures. Nixon's secretary, Rose Woods, testified that she was responsible for one erasure: While transcribing the tape, she said, she had inadvertently pressed the "record" button and thus created a five-minute gap. That left quite a bit to be explained and no respectable theory to explain it.

On April 11, the Judiciary Committee of the House of Representatives, tired of waiting for Nixon's tapes, issued a subpoena—a formal legal demand—for the tapes of 42 conversations, to be delivered by the end of the month. Still defiant, Nixon refused to turn over the actual tapes, instead turning over typed transcripts of the portions that he himself considered relevant to the Watergate investigation. In addressing the nation on April 29, the evening before he released the transcripts, Nixon claimed that he did not learn of the Watergate cover-up until March 21, 1973—nearly nine months after the burglary. He also claimed, "after March 21, my actions were directed toward finding the facts and seeing that justice was done fairly and according to the law."

Near the conclusion of his televised speech, Nixon expressed his hopes that the transcripts would end the matter and show that he was blameless: "I was trying . . . to discover what was right and to do what was right. I hope, and I trust, that, when you have seen the evidence

in its entirety, you will see the truth of that statement." Unfortunately for the President, the transcripts did little to satisfy the public or the House Judiciary Committee. Three major problems led to continuing suspicion. First, Nixon had refused to turn over the actual tapes and had edited out portions of the tapes when preparing the transcripts. The second problem was that there were many other tapes that he had not turned over. Finally, the problem remained of the 18½-minute gap on a tape that many felt was crucial to discovering the truth.

The courts and Congress continued their attempts to gain full access to Nixon's tapes, and on July 24, 1974, the U.S. Supreme Court ruled against Nixon, deciding that executive privilege did not protect him from being required to turn over the tapes. Although Nixon had battled the Watergate scandal for over two years, the Supreme Court's decision would make it impossible for

Investigators suspected that key aspects of the Watergate affair had been discussed in the Oval Office. When they learned that President Nixon kept tape recordings of many of his conversations, the special prosecutor on the case subpoenaed the tapes. After much reluctance and debate, Nixon released the tapes. However, many critical pieces of conversation seemed to have been altered or deleted.

him to keep fighting. One tape in particular finally gave the court, Congress, and the public definitive proof that Nixon was personally involved in covering up the burglary that had been funded by his campaign to spy on the Democratic candidates.

The tape made on June 23, 1972—less than a week after the burglary—became known as the "smoking gun" tape. Like a smoking gun in a criminal's hand, the tape provided indisputable evidence of Nixon's wrongdoing. According to a transcript of the tape, President Nixon himself asked his trusted aide H.R. Haldeman to meet with CIA officials and tell them "that they should call the FBI in and say that we wish for the country, don't go any further into this case . . ."

With evidence that he had participated in the cover-up from the very beginning and had lied to the American public ever since, it became clear that Congress would eventually remove Nixon from office through the process of impeachment, a process begun by the House Judiciary Committee. According to the Constitution, the House of Representatives may impeach—charge with an offense that warrants removal from office—the president and other federal officials. If the House votes to impeach the president, then the Senate decides whether or not to convict the president: a two-thirds majority is needed for conviction. If convicted, the President is removed from office and may be subjected to criminal charges by the court system.

Although the House Judiciary Committee recommended to the House of Representatives that they impeach Nixon, the full House never had a chance to vote. On August 8, 1974, Nixon addressed a television audience from the Oval Office, saying that although he did not want to leave office, he had decided to resign because it was in the country's best interest to move past the Watergate scandal. The next day, Nixon formally resigned as president, and Gerald Ford of Michigan was sworn in as the 38th president of the United States.

Although Nixon had finally been defeated, he signaled "V" for victory with both hands raised above his head as he left the White House lawn by helicopter.

Despite widespread speculation of a criminal trial, Richard Nixon never faced criminal charges. On September 8, 1974, President Ford exercised his presidential powers to pardon Nixon of any crimes that he might have committed. Although many people were angry and felt that Nixon should face charges, the Watergate scandal was finally over for Richard Nixon.

Nixon's resignation started a new chapter in American history, in which the activities of the president would be subject to greater public scrutiny. As the years passed, for example, Ronald Reagan would have to deal with the "Iran-Contra Affair," a scandal that involved secret

Under the threat of impeachment, Nixon resigned the office of President in the summer of 1974, leaving the White House in the Presidential helicopter for the final time.

Nixon's successor, former Vice President Gerald Ford, moved quickly to put the Watergate scandal in the past. By granting Richard Nixon a full pardon, he ended any hopes of prosecuting the former leader. Ford's decision still remains controversial.

arms sales to the enemy nation of Iran. However, Reagan finished out his two terms as president and was never directly tied to the scandal. In 1998, the House of Representatives impeached Bill Clinton—a fate that Nixon had escaped through his resignation. However, Clinton remained in office after the Senate found him not guilty of the charges relating to his cover-up of an affair with White House intern Monica Lewinsky. As the 20th century ended, Richard Nixon remained the only president ever forced to leave office, and it all started with a piece of tape on a doorway.

Ironically, Liddy, the bright former FBI agent who helped to coordinate the Watergate burglary, could have prevented the discovery of the tape. The burglars told Liddy that the guard had discovered the tape, but Liddy allowed the operation to continue. He recalls:

> I knew that lock-taping was a common, if disapproved, practice of maintenance personnel in large buildings. That should not have alarmed the guard, who could be expected to remove it. I saw no reason that the guard should think anything other than that the maintenance people would have to be lectured.
>
> I had no idea that McCord was going to retape the locks.

Thanks to an alert security guard, history was changed forever.

Chronology

September 1901: President William McKinley is assassinated by anarchist Leon Czolgosz.

April 1920: Two men are murdered in a robbery in South Braintree, Massachusetts. Nicolo Sacco and Bartolomeo Vanzetti, two anarchists and Italian immigrants, are later arrested.

July 1921: Sacco and Vanzetti are convicted of murder.

May 1924: A 14-year-old boy is murdered in Chicago. Nathan Leopold, Jr., and Richard Loeb, two teenagers from wealthy families are later arrested.

July 1924: Leopold and Loeb plead guilty to murder; they later would each be sentenced to life in prison, plus 99 years.

August 1927: Sacco and Vanzetti are executed, leading to demonstrations and labor strikes in the U.S. and overseas.

February 1929: Al Capone's gang kills seven rivals during the "St. Valentine's Day Massacre."

March 1930: Bonnie Parker helps Clyde Barrow escape from a Texas jail.

December 1930: Charles "Pretty Boy" Floyd escapes from a prison train.

February 1932: Clyde Barrow is paroled from a Texas prison.

March 1932: The son of famous aviator Charles Lindbergh is kidnapped from the family residence.

November 1932: "Pretty Boy" Floyd robs a bank in his hometown of Sallisaw, Oklahoma, in broad daylight.

April 1933: Bonnie and Clyde's gang kill two Missouri State Troopers in a shootout.

June 1933: Four lawmen and their prisoner are gunned down in front of a train station during the "Kansas City Massacre." Floyd is later named a prime suspect.

September 1933: John Dillinger is arrested for bank robbery.

October 1933: Members of John Dillinger's gang spring him from a Lima, Ohio, jail.

Chronology

January 1934: Bonnie and Clyde spring gang member Raymond Hamilton and others during a raid on a prison farm. John Dillinger is arrested for bank robbery and murder.

March 1934: John Dillinger escapes from jail and joins forces with Homer Van Meter and "Baby Face Nelson" (Lester Gillis)

April 1934: Dillinger, Van Meter, and Nelson escape shootout with FBI agents.

May 1934: Former Texas Ranger Frank Hamer leads ambush that kills Bonnie and Clyde.

June 1934: John Dillinger becomes nation's first "Public Enemy Number One."

July 1934: Chicago FBI agent Melvin Purvis leads ambush that kills Dillinger.

August 1934: Federal prisoners begin to arrive at new penitentiary on Alcatraz.

October 1934: Purvis leads ambush that kills Floyd.

November 1934: Chicago FBI agents kill Baby Face Nelson.

January 1950: Armed robbers steal over $2 million from Brink's building in Boston.

June 1959: Julius and Ethel Rosenberg, a married couple, are executed for spying for the Soviet Union.

June 1962: Frank Lee Morris, John Anglin, and Clarence Anglin escape from Alcatraz.

March 1963: Bureau of Prisons closes penitentiary on Alcatraz.

June 1963: Civil rights leader Medgar Evers is assassinated.

November 1963: President John F. Kennedy is assassinated.

February 1965: Civil rights leader Malcolm X is assassinated.

April 1968: Civil rights leader Martin Luther King, Jr., is assassinated.

Chronology

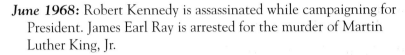

June 1968: Robert Kennedy is assassinated while campaigning for President. James Earl Ray is arrested for the murder of Martin Luther King, Jr.

March 1969: James Earl Ray pleads guilty to the murder of Martin Luther King, Jr.

August 1969: The Charles Manson "family" brutally murders actress Sharon Tate and four others.

June 1972: Five men break into the headquarters of the Democratic National Committee in the Watergate building.

July 1974: President Richard Nixon releases tape recording proving that he knew about the Watergate burglary and tried to cover up the White House's involvement.

August 1974: Richard Nixon resigns as President in the wake of the Watergate scandal.

July 1976: First in a series of "Son of Sam" murders in New York City.

August 1977: David Berkowitz is arrested and charged with "Son of Sam" killings.

December 1980: Musician John Lennon is assassinated.

March 1981: President Ronald Reagan survives assassination attempt by John Hinckley, Jr.

February 1993: Terrorists bomb World Trade Center, killing six people.

June 1994: Nicole Brown and Ronald Goldman are murdered in Los Angeles. Football star O.J. Simpson, Brown's ex-husband, flees police in a nationally televised chase.

January 1995: Murder trial of O.J. Simpson opens in the courtroom of Judge Lance Ito.

April 1995: A bomb explodes at a federal building in Oklahoma City. Timothy McVeigh is later convicted for the crime.

October 1995: O.J. Simpson is found not guilty of murders of Ronald Goldman and Nicole Brown.

Further Reading

Bruns, Roger A. *The Bandit Kings: From Jesse James to Pretty Boy Floyd*. New York: Crown Publishers, 1995.

David, Andrew. *Famous Criminal Trials*. Minneapolis: Lerner Publications, 1979.

George, Linda. *Alcatraz*. New York: Children's Press, 1998.

Haskins, James. *The Life and Death of Martin Luther King, Jr.* New York: Beech Tree Books, 1992.

Kilian, Pamela. *What Was Watergate? A Young Reader's Guide to Understanding an Era*. New York: St. Martin's Press, 1990.

Bibliography

Babyak, Jolene. *Breaking the Rock: The Great Escape from Alcatraz*. Berkeley, Calif.: Ariel Vamp Press, 2001.

Bernstein, Carl and Bob Woodward. *All the President's Men*. New York: Simon and Schuster, 1974.

Bruns, Roger A. *The Bandit Kings: From Jesse James to Pretty Boy Floyd*. New York: Crown Publishers, 1995.

Bugliosi, Vincent. *Outrage: The Five Reasons Why O.J. Simpson Got Away with Murder*. New York: W.W. Norton & Co., 1996.

Cromie, Robert and Joseph Pinkston. *Dillinger: A Short and Violent Life*. New York: McGraw-Hill, 1962.

Federal Bureau of Investigation. *Charles "Pretty Boy" Floyd Summary*. Washington, D.C.: Federal Bureau of Investigation, undated.

Federal Bureau of Investigation. *John Anglin, Clarence Anglin, and Frank Lee Morris Escape from Alcatraz, File No. 76-26295*. Washington, D.C.: Federal Bureau of Investigation, undated.

Frankfurter, Felix. *The Case of Sacco and Vanzetti: A Critical Analysis for Lawyers and Laymen*. Boston: Little, Brown, 1927.

Frankfurter, Marion Denman and Gardner Jackson, eds. *The Letters of Sacco and Vanzetti*. New York: Viking, 1928

Gaddis, Thomas E., *Birdman of Alcatraz: The Story of Robert Stroud*. New York: Signet Books, 1962.

Garment, Leonard. *In Search of Deep Throat: The Greatest Political Mystery of Our Time*. New York: Basic Books, 2000.

Girardin, G. Russell and William J. Helmer. *Dillinger: The Untold Story*. Bloomington, Ind.: Indiana University Press, 1994.

Gold, Gerald, ed. *The White House Transcripts: The full Text of the Submission of Recorded Presidential Conversations to the Committee on the Judiciary of the House of Representatives by President Richard Nixon*. New York: Bantam Books, 1974.

Higdon, Hal. *Leopold and Loeb: The Crime of the Century*. Urbana, Ill., University of Chicago Press, 1999.

Johnston, James A. *Alcatraz Island Prison and the Men Who Live There*. New York: Charles Scribners' Sons, 1949.

King, Martin L., Jr., *March on Washington, 1963*. *http://www.thekingcenter.org/mlk/bio.html*.

Lange, Tom, Philip Vannatter, and Dan E. Moldea. *Evidence Dismissed: The Inside Story of the Police Investigation of O.J. Simpson.* New York: Pocket Books, 1997.

Leopold, Nathan F., Jr., *Life Plus 99 Years.* Garden City, N.Y.: Doubleday, 1958.

Liddy, G. Gordon. *Will: The Autobiography of G. Gordon Liddy.* New York: St. Martin's, 1980.

Livesey, Robert. *On the Rock—Twenty-Five Years in Alcatraz: The Prison Story of Alvin Karpis as Told to Robert Livesey.* New York: Beaufort, 1980.

Milner, E.R. *The Lives and Times of Bonnie and Clyde.* Carbondale, Ill.: Southern Illinois University Press, 1996.

National Archives and Records Administration. *Transcript of Audiotape Dated June 23, 1972.* Washington, D.C., National Archives and Records Administration, undated.

Odier, Pierre. *The Rock: A History of Alcatraz the Fort/the Prison.* Eagle Rock, Calif.: L'Image Odier, 1982.

Phillips, John Neal. *Running with Bonnie and Clyde: The Ten Fast Years of Ralph Fults.* Norman, Okla.: University of Oklahoma Press, 1996.

Posner, Gerald. *Killing the Dream: James Earl Ray and the Assassination of Martin Luther King, Jr.* New York: Random House, 1998.

Russell, Francis. *Sacco and Vanzetti: The Case Resolved.* New York: Harper & Row, 1986.

Schulke, Flip and Penelope O. McPhee. *King Remembered.* New York: W.W. Norton & Co., 1986.

Steele, Phillip W. and Marie Barrow Scoma. *The Family Story of Bonnie and Clyde.* Gretna, La.: Pelican Publishing Co., 2000.

Sussman, Barry. *The Great Cover-up: Nixon and the Scandal of Watergate.* New York: Thomas Y. Crowell Co., 1974

Toland, John. *The Dillinger Days.* New York: Random House, 1963.

Treherne, John. *The Strange History of Bonnie and Clyde.* London: Jonathan Cape, 1984.

United States Department of Justice. *Report of the Department of Justice Task Force to Review the FBI Martin Luther King, Jr., Security and Assassination Investigations.* Washington, D.C.: United States Department of Justice, January 11, 1977.

Wallis, Michael. *Pretty Boy: The Life and Times of Charles Arthur Floyd.* New York: St. Martin's Press, 1992.

Young, William and David E. Kaiser. *Postmortem: New Evidence in the Case of Sacco and Vanzetti.* Amherst, Mass.: University of Massachusetts Press, 1985.

Index

Index

Index

Picture Credits

ALAN MARZILLI studied law at Georgetown University and English at Emory University. He currently lives in Durham, North Carolina, where he writes about mental health policy and other subjects.

AUSTIN SARAT is William Nelson Cromwell Professor of Jurisprudence and Political Science at Amherst College, where he also chairs the Department of Law, Jurisprudence and Social Thought. Professor Sarat is the author or editor of 23 books and numerous scholarly articles. Among his books are *Law's Violence, Sitting in Judgment: Sentencing the White Collar Criminal*, and *Justice and Injustice in Law and Legal Theory*. He has received many academic awards and held several prestigious fellowships. He is President of the Law & Society Association and Chair of the Working Group on Law, Culture and the Humanities. In addition, he is a nationally recognized teacher and educator whose teaching has been featured in the *New York Times*, on the *Today* show, and on National Public Radio's *Fresh Air*.